英 語 の 文 法 と 語 法 を 理 解 す る

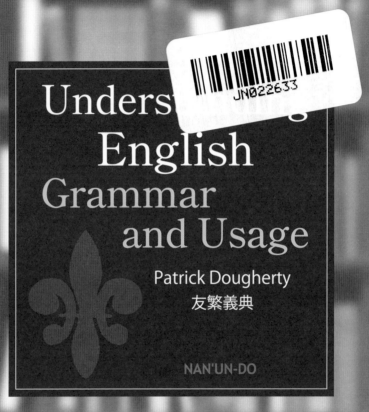

Understanding English Grammar and Usage

Patrick Dougherty
友繁義典

NAN'UN-DO

音声ファイル
無料 DL
のご案内

このテキストの音声を無料で視聴（ストリーミング）・ダウンロード
できます。自習用音声としてご活用ください。
以下のサイトにアクセスしてテキスト番号で検索してください。

https://nanun-do.com　テキスト番号［**512225**］

※ 無線 LAN（WiFi）に接続してのご利用を推奨いたします。

※ 音声ダウンロードは Zip ファイルでの提供になります。
　お使いの機器によっては別途ソフトウェア（アプリケーション）
　の導入が必要となります。

Read by
Ryan Drees
Jennifer Skidmore

※ Understanding English Grammar and Usage 音声ダウンロードページは
以下の QR コードからもご利用になれます。

INTRODUCTION

"The greater part of the world's troubles are due to questions of grammar." ~ Michel de Montaigne

"Grammar," for many, is a frightening word. It connotes perplexing rules that must be memorized to pass even more perplexing tests. This is unfortunate, as grammar itself is simply a search for clarity and order. Grammar builds a base upon which meaning can be constructed and communication successfully achieved. In the parlance of the United Kingdom and the United States, the first formal level of education was historically called the "grammar school." It served as the foundation of education. The choice of words is poetic in a way, as grammar is the foundation of language. Perhaps the problem has been one of how the words and phrases have been presented to the reader. Discussion of grammar often revolves around opaque descriptions of usage with a frustratingly high incidence of obscure terminology. What *Understanding English Grammar and Usage* works to accomplish is ease of understanding. A number of complex grammar questions are addressed with clear, concise, and layperson friendly answers. The selection of questions was done with the ambition of addressing the most challenging grammatical concepts that haunt the student of the English language. Accessibility is the objective with each of the answers. This book is meant for the student and for the language aficionado.

Patrick Dougherty and Yoshinori Tomoshige

HOW TO USE THIS TEXTBOOK

Meant for any serious exploration of English grammar, this textbook was designed for both classroom use and self-study. Each unit involves an in-depth question, or questions, about complex English grammar. After the question section there is a response where each question receives a clear, definitive, answer. After the question-and-answer sections there are exercises where the student of grammar may then apply their new understanding to solve various word and sentence problems utilizing the information provided regarding the grammar under study. Through this process of question and answer and then application of understanding, the student of grammar will, step by step, improve their understanding of complex English grammar.

CONTENTS

INTRODUCTION 3

HOW TO USE THIS TEXTBOOK 4

CONTENTS 5

Unit 1 Articles 6

Unit 2 Modal Auxiliaries 10

Unit 3 Adverbs 14

Unit 4 Conjunctions 18

Unit 5 Prepositions (part 1) 22

Unit 6 Prepositions (part 2) 26

Unit 7 Prepositions (part 3) 30

Unit 8 Countable and Uncountable Nouns 34

Unit 9 Formal and Informal Expressions 38

Unit 10 Expressions Referring to "Future Time" 42

Unit 11 Expressions of Reason and Cause 46

Unit 12 "If ... not" and "Unless" 50

Unit 13 Causative Verbs 54

Unit 14 Middle Constructions 58

Unit 15 Negative Expressions 62

Unit 16 Passive Constructions 66

Unit 17 Present Perfect Forms 70

Unit 18 Possessive Constructions 74

Unit 19 Existential Sentences 78

Unit 20 Simple Forms of Verbs and Progressive Forms of Verbs 82

Articles

QUESTION

⌂ ♪02

In our English conversation class, our American teacher asked me what type of animal I would like to own as a pet. So, I said to him "I'd like to have dog." Then he laughed out loud, but I didn't know the reason for his laughter, so I asked him why he laughed, but he just smiled at me and wrote the following statements (a) and (b) and told me to guess the difference between them. But since there are no articles in Japanese, it is hard for me to tell (a) from (b). So, could you tell me the difference between them?

> **(a) I'd like to have a dog.**
> **(b) I'd like to have dog.**

ANSWER

⌂ ♪03

In the noun phrase "a dog," "a" is an indefinite article. We use it when we refer to a noun that is not specific. I could say, "I like a good book," this means that any good book would do and that I would be happy reading any book that I found that was good. If I said, "I like the book," then I am referring to a specific book. For example, someone could ask me, "Do you like the new textbook that our professor wrote?" and, if I did, I would respond, "Yes, I like the book."

With regard to example (a), "I'd like to have a dog," you could use that when you were asked, for example, what type of animal you might like to own as a pet. You could have responded, "When it comes to pets, I like a dog." Now, why did your English teacher laugh when you said "I'd like to have dog?" He laughed because it was the form that is often used when referring to the type of food, or dish, one likes to eat. For example, if someone asked "What is your favorite meal?" I could respond, "I like barbeque," or "I like pasta." When you responded, "I'd like to have dog," it sounded like you were referring to what you liked to eat. I am sure that that is not what was meant.

In this connection, if we say "I'd like to have dogs," it means although there are various kinds of dogs, I like any dogs. And, with regard to a sentence like "I love that dog," we refer to a specific dog and the dog is known to both the speaker and hearer. And lastly, as for the sentences like "I love that dog," we are talking about one specific dog among some dogs.

ANOTHER QUESTION

⌂ ♪04

I understand that as you explain, an indefinite article is used to refer to non-specific nouns, but I think that an indefinite article may also be used to mention a specific noun.

For example, if some person says, "I'd like to consult a lawyer," he or she may have a specific lawyer in his or her mind, but it might be possible that he or she is referring to a non-specific lawyer, too. This sentence could be used to express that he or she would like to consult any lawyer as long as the person is any type of lawyer. This means the expression "a lawyer" can refer to both a specific noun and a non-specific one. Therefore, it seems that there are cases where an indefinite article is also used to refer to a specific noun. So, we need to consider sentences such as "I like a good book," and "I'd like to consult a lawyer," and distinguish the former type and the latter type properly. How would you explain the cases where these types of sentences actually occur?

ANOTHER ANSWER

05

Yes, you are correct that the speaker could be referring to a specific lawyer. However, we would only really know that via the context of the conversation. Let's say two men are at a party. A woman who is a medical doctor walks up and talks with them. After she leaves, one of the men looks at the other and says, "I'd like to marry a doctor." In that context the man might very well be referring to the woman doctor that just spoke to them. It would only be understood via the tone and facial expressions of the individual saying it, and would entirely be dependent on this bit of body language and the context for us to be sure what was meant. Language requires more than words to make sense. We need context and other clues to perceive meaning. That would be the only method that we would be able to employ in order to understand if a specific person or thing was meant.

Taking this discussion further, when it is an issue of determining whether a specific doctor or dog or cat or another entity is being referred to by the speaker, the entity must be indicated by the speaker or writer and this is often done contextually. For example, if a child walked into a room and saw some chocolate bars on a table and exclaimed, "I want candy," we would know from the context that the child wants the candy (chocolate bars) on the table. This kind of information is obtained from the context and from the circumstances of the scene.

So, if we use the indefinite article "a" or "an," it will always refer to a non-specific noun unless the context and other factors play a part to hint to the listener or reader that a specific noun is being referred to in the conversation or statement. Language works within a structure of context and association. Basically, when we try to understand the meaning of some expression containing an article, we always have to consider the context in which the expression occurs. However, as a general rule, we can usually rely on the simple structure of "the" referring to a specific category and "a/an" referring to a general category.

Exercise 1

Put an appropriate article in the blank. If no article is necessary, leave the blank empty.

1. I have a lot of friends. Most of them are (   ) company employees.

2. When I was (   ) high school student, I belonged to the tennis club.

3. Jane says she would like to be (   ) actress.

4. George is (   ) lawyer. His parents were (   ) lawyers, too.

5. Bye! Have (   ) nice weekend.

6. What (   ) coincidence! I wasn't expecting to see you here.

7. Is he (   ) nice person?

8. I think he will be (   ) good teacher.

9. Nature is (   ) best physician.

10. Sally is (   ) excellent dancer.

11. Would you like (   ) cup of coffee?

12. They live in (   ) big house in the middle of town.

13. (   ) hotel where we stayed was very nice.

14. He seems to have (   ) problem. I think I'll try to be of some help.

15. Room 17 is on (   ) third floor.

16. Just when I got (   ) home, it began to rain.

17. I hear Joe was in (   ) prison for robbery for two years.

18. We must admit that it's hard to get (   ) regular job these days.

19. Only (   ) superrich could afford a mansion like that.

20. What time do you usually go to (   ) work?

21. John loves to look at (   ) stars in (   ) sky.

22. (   ) earth goes around (   ) sun.

23. She doesn't watch (   ) TV much, but listens to (   ) radio a lot.

24. He's a vegetarian. He never eats (   ) meat.

25. What time did you go to (   ) bed last night?

26. I can play the tune without (   ) sheet music.

27. After he told the joke, there was (   ) burst of laughter.

28. I think you'd better go to (   ) dentist.

29. Let's go to the station by (   ) taxi.

30. John kissed her on (   ) cheek.

Exercise 2

Choose the right one.

1. Why don't we go to (movies / the movies) tonight?

2. Have you had (dinner / the dinner) yet, George?

3. What would you like to have for (breakfast / the breakfast)?

4. It's difficult to imagine life without (Internet / the Internet) nowadays.

5. John had (big lunch / a big lunch) at noon.

6. She has always been good. She has never been in (trouble / the trouble).

7. Do you have a car, or will you use (public transportation / the public transportation)?

8. (Art / The art) is long, (life / the life) is short.

9. (Tea / The tea) I had after dinner was very good.

10. I would like to see (Professor Smith / the Professor Smith).

Exercise 3

Complete the sentences using the words given in the square brackets and then translate them into Japanese.

1. [we, yesterday, the, met, girl, name, that, of, what's]?

   _____?

   Japanese _____

2. [I, five, eight, a, a, work, day, and, days, week, hours].

   _____.

   Japanese _____

3. [John, the, still, is, with, in, flu, bed].

   _____.

   Japanese _____

4. [keeps, doctor, apple, day, a, an, the, away].

   _____.

   Japanese _____

Modal Auxiliaries

QUESTION
 06

   I wrote this sentence "I made a mad dash and could catch the last train," and I showed it to an American friend of mine and he said that I should rewrite it like "I made a mad dash and was able to catch the last train." I thought "be able to" and "can" were synonymous and in this context, you were always exchangeable. So, I asked him the difference between them, but he said he could not explain the difference properly but that he just knew that in this sentence we should use "was able to" but not "could." So, could you tell me the exact difference between the following (a) and (b)?

> **(a) I made a mad dash and could catch the last train.**
> **(b) I made a mad dash and was able to catch the last train.**

ANSWER
 07

   These two, "could" and "was able to," are *usually* interchangeable. However, in this case, "could" indicates a state of possibility whereas "was able to" indicates that something actually did happen. Sentence (b) tells the reader or listener that you *did* catch the last train. If you said, "I made a mad dash and could catch the last train," it does not tell us that you actually got on the train, but only that you were there in time to catch the last train. Grammatically, the word "could" is a modal auxiliary verb. It is the form of the past-tense of the word "can," and it is used to describe possibility or an ability to do something in the past. It should not be used in sentences where you describe an ability to do something at one moment in time. For example, "Last week I could run a kilometer in under six minutes," is not grammatically correct because the sentence denotes a single past action. We can only use "could" for general statements, such as "When I was in high school, I could run two kilometers in under ten minutes." If we must refer to a specific occasion, then we have to use the past form of "be able to" which is "was able to." Just remember that "was able to" is used in place of "could" in situations where you are referring to a specific occasion. For example, "Last Tuesday I was able to connect to the Internet for the first time." Another example would be, "On June 5th, last year, I was able to graduate from high school." And remember that "could" is used for general statements about past ability that was repeated or repeatable, such as "During my college days I could study for ten hours straight." Also remember that "was able to" should be used when you refer to past ability and make reference to a specific time and event. It tells the reader that not only did you have the ability; you used the ability to achieve something. For example, you would say, "The day before my final examinations in college, I was able to study for ten straight hours to get ready for my mathematics examination."

ANOTHER QUESTION

From your explanation, I understand that when you refer to a past event that actually happened, we need to use "was [were] able to" but not "could." So "actuality" may be a key word to deal with what we have seen so far. Therefore, in expressing a negative event in a past-tense context "could" can be used with a negative expression such as "I made a mad dash but couldn't catch the last train." Am I correct in this regard?

ANOTHER ANSWER

Yes, if you use the expression "I made a mad dash but couldn't catch the last train," you would be correct in your usage. When you express a negative event in a past-tense context, you would be able to use either "was not able to" or "could not." The circumstances are clear: you were not able to get on a train even though you rushed to the train station. The important point in this is that the language needs to be clear enough to make the reader or listener understand what occurred. If you, in the reverse, had been able to catch the train after your dash, you cannot say that "I made a mad dash and could catch the last train." Now, some would argue that this is being too worried about being exact, but if you truly want to make sure that everyone understands your meaning you cannot use "could" in that situation. Why? This is what students often ask. They feel that I am being too worried about the exactness of meaning. Well, I am a teacher and a linguist, and that means it is my business to be concerned about making sure that statements truly mean what they are meant to mean. So, why is "couldn't" appropriate in this statement, "I made a mad dash but couldn't catch the last train?"

The word "could" indicates the ability to do something but does not indicate that something was actually done, or the goal accomplished. To be more precise, in the past tense "could" does not normally have the implication of actuality if there is reference to a single action in the past, while the negative form "couldn't" clearly denies the actuality of the event. Therefore, the statement "I made a mad dash but couldn't catch the last train" is perfectly grammatical. And if there is not an indication of a single action, but of a repeated or habitual action, "could" can be employed, even if there is an implication that the action did take place. So, for example, I could say, "My wife could swim for one hour when she was in high school." Moreover, the past tense form "could" is normal when it is used with verbs of sensation as in "I could see the stars," or "I could hear her voice clearly."

Exercise 1

Complete the sentences using *can* or *be able to*.

1. Jane has lived in Paris for three years. She (   ) speak French.

2. Jane has lived in Paris for three years, so she should (   ) speak French.

3. Tom used to (   ) stand on his hands, but he can't do it anymore.

4. I (   ) see you on Saturday if you like.

5. Kate might (   ) visit us tomorrow.

Exercise 2

Put *can*, *can't*, *could*, or *couldn't* in the blanks to complete the sentences.

1. I'm afraid I (   ) help you with your work.

2. I was shocked to hear the news. I (   ) believe it.

3. You (   ) see the hotel next to the bank, if you turn right at that intersection.

4. I'm not in a hurry. It (   ) wait.

5. When James was a boy, he (   ) swim very well.

6. I wish I (   ) play the violin like that violinist.

7. For the life of me, I (   ) remember her name.

8. You (   ) get a driver's license until you are 18 in Japan.

9. I (   ) go to the party because I had a cold.

10. The room was so silent. You (   ) hear a pin drop.

Exercise 3

Fill in the blanks with the most appropriate words given below.

[may, don't have to, can't, can't, should, should, should, should, must, must, mustn't, might]

1. **A:** Who was the girl we saw John with last night?

   B: I'm not sure. She (   ) have been his sister.

2. **A:** Shall we walk to the station?

   B: (   ) as well.

3. You (   ) attend the meeting. I can attend it alone.

4. You must be tired. You (   ) go to bed now.

5. Did you miss watching the baseball game last night? You (   ) have watched it. It was very exciting!

6. I can't find my wallet. I (   ) have dropped it somewhere.

7. Everyone (   ) know the rule.

8. He's been working all day. He (   ) be tired.

9. He's an honest person. He (   ) have told such a lie.

10. It is natural that she (   ) complain about her salary.

11. This is a secret. You (   ) tell anyone.

12. She has just had dinner. She (   ) be hungry now.

Exercise 4

Complete the sentences using the words given in the square brackets and translate them into Japanese.

1. I [wanted, the rock, to, really, to, go, concert], but I [ticket, get, couldn't, a].

   I _____ **, but I** _____ .

   Japanese _____

2. [your, on, congratulations, promotion]. [very, must, be, you, pleased].

   _____ .

   Japanese _____

   _____ .

   Japanese _____

3. If [of, might, some, you, I, have, some, be, problem, help].

   If _____ .

   Japanese _____

4. You look sick. [drunk, much, you, have, shouldn't, so].

   You look sick. _____ .

   Japanese _____

Adverbs

QUESTION

🎧 10

I have learned that "about" and "around" are both prepositions and adverbs and their meanings are often the same. For example, with regard to "John walked about the pond," and "John walked around the pond," these sentences refer to the same situation. But I hear that "about" and "around" sometimes can be different. How about the following (a) and (b) sentences?

> **(a) Little Jenny is running about the backyard.**
> **(b) Little Jenny is running around the backyard.**

ANSWER

🎧 11

You are right that the two words are usually able to be used interchangeably in many cases. Indeed, often the choice of one word or the other is up to simple preference or is due to the difference between British English and American English, as the use of "about" as can be seen in "John walked about the pond" being a phrase that would be more common in England, and "John walked around the pond" being more common in America. However, there are cases where the terms are not interchangeable, and I will give you some examples. If I were describing the circumference of a circle, I would say, "The circle is 30 centimeters around." But I would *not* be able to say, "The circle is 30 centimeters about." There are also cases of "about" being used as a preposition, in such situations as someone mentioning the topic of a film, such as "The film was about a famous samurai." I could not say, "The film was around a famous samurai." That would be incorrect. Also, we can use the word "about" to ask what something deals with, as in the example, "Tell me what the film is about." We cannot say, "Tell me what the film is around." That also would be incorrect. Likewise, we should not use "about" when we are referring to the basis, or center, of some activity. For example, we would say, "The story is based around an account of a World War I battle." However, we cannot say, "The story is based about an account of a World War I battle." When "about" is used as an adverb, there are also times that it is not interchangeable with "around." For example, when speaking of the time till something is prepared, as in "Lunch is about ready." We cannot say, "Lunch is around ready." Likewise, we cannot use "about" when asking someone to return to visit us again, as in "Please come about again." We should use, "Please come around again." That usage would be correct.

ANOTHER QUESTION

I know each word can be used as an adverb denoting distance, time or the amount of money such as

> (a) **What time is it now? It's about five.**
> (b) **What time is it now? It's around five.**
> (c) **How far is it from here? It's about five miles.**
> (d) **How far is it from here? It's around five miles.**

Are there any differences between (a), (c) and (b), (d) if any?

ANOTHER ANSWER

Good question, and, yes, there are differences. Let me explain. There is a difference between using the term "about" and the term "around." Let's look at the first set of examples, those dealing with time. If you say, as you did, "It's about five," this means that it is near to five o'clock but has not yet reached five o'clock. Basically, it is any close time up to five o'clock. For example, it could be 4:49. However, it can never be beyond five o'clock. It can't be 5:01, for example. On the other hand, if you use "around" as in "It is around five o'clock," you mean that the time is close to five o'clock and, with this being a key point, it could be a bit after five o'clock. In other words, it could be soon before five o'clock or soon after five o'clock. In other words, it could be 4:55 or 5:05. Either interpretation would be fine.

Likewise, when we look at the second set, the ones that deal with distance, the same principle applies. If I say "It is about five miles from here" I mean that it is just short of five miles. But if I say "It is around five miles from here," I mean that it could be a little less or a little more than five miles from here.

These are the technical sides of the use of "about" and "around." Though, in daily use, you will frequently find people making errors in their use, especially when speaking. However, understanding the difference will give you an added advantage in communication.

Exercise 1

Complete the sentences with *about* or *around*.

1. This special property is fenced all (   ).

2. It's (   ) time to go to bed.

3. They traveled (   ) the world in 2023.

4. I bet I'll see you (   ).

5. I'm (   ) done with it.

Exercise 2

Translate the following sentences into Japanese.

1. All of a sudden, he stopped walking and looked around.

   Japanese _____

2. The pond is about 800 meters around.

   Japanese _____

3. He is one of the best painters around.

   Japanese _____

4. The flies were going around and around in circles.

   Japanese _____

5. My work is about finished.

   Japanese _____

6. The kids were running around in the yard.

   Japanese _____

7. When I went into the room, strangely enough, there were several people lying about on the floor.

   Japanese _____

8. The small children were running about barefoot on the beach.

   Japanese _____

9. There were several young people hanging about on the street corner.

   Japanese _____

10. There was a lot of flu about last year.

    Japanese _____

11. I'm not about to talk about the matter again.

Japanese _____

Exercise 3

Fill in the blanks using the words given below so that the second sentence can have the same meaning as the first one. [abroad, in, indoors, away]

1. Is George at home?

Is George (   )?

2. John is on holiday at the moment.

John is (   ) at the moment.

3. John is making a trip to a foreign country.

John is making a trip (   ).

4. Let's go into the building.

Let's go (   ).

Exercise 4

Rewrite each sentence so that it contains a word given below. Each word is used only once. [in, indoors, outside, away, abroad]

1. Let's go into the house now.

_____

2. Sam has gone on a trip.

_____

3. John has gone to live in a foreign country.

_____

4. Don't come in, please.

_____

5. Sorry, but Kenny isn't at home at the moment.

_____

Conjunctions

🎧14

QUESTION

I know that both "although" and "though" are used to express a contrast with the idea in a main clause and that they can be exchangeable in many cases. But would you tell me exactly in what situation(s) is each conjunction properly used? Moreover, I find that the word "though" is often employed at the end of a sentence. Could you explain how to use it correctly?

> (a) **Although I was tired, I kept on working.**
> (b) **Though I was tired, I kept on working.**
> (c) **I kept working. I was tired, though.**

ANSWER

🎧15

Generally, "although" and "though" are synonymous. The two words can be used interchangeably when they are used as conjunctions. However, there are some differences in where and how the words can, and are, used. Let's first focus on the word "although." As "though" is often thought to be merely a shortened version of "although" this is a good place to start. "Although" is often thought to be more emphatic, or more energetic than "though." Take this sentence, for example, "Although he still loses most of the time, the man does not give up trying." This puts more emphasis on the man's willingness to keep trying even in the face of defeat. Another example of this would be this sentence: "Although he is afraid of flying, he decided to fly to France to see his daughter graduate from college."

Another difference is that the word "although" is most commonly found at the beginning of a clause. For example, the speaker or writer might say, "Although they are very similar, the two brothers have some differences," or, "Although he hated to travel, he still decided to join his son on his trip to New Zealand." "Although" doesn't have the ability to move to the end of a clause, as the word "though" does. For example, you cannot say, "He cannot run fast, although." However, you can say, "He cannot run fast, though." "Although" must stay at the beginning of any clause in which it is used. "Though" has the ability to be used at the beginning or at the end of a clause.

Another difference between "although" and "though" is that you cannot use "although" to intensify questions or statements. For example, you cannot respond to a statement such as, "It's a very tall mountain," by saying, "Isn't it, although?" You can, however, say, "Isn't it, though?" The use of "though" at the end of this clause acts as something of a pause for effect.

We have discussed some special characteristics of the word "though;" however, there are a few more points that are special to "though" that separate it from "although."

For example, "though" can be used with the adverb "even" as in the sentence, "Even though he was short, he decided to try out for the school basketball team." You cannot do this with the word "although," as in "Even although he could not swim well, he decided to go out for the school swim team." The word "Even" will only work with the word "though."

So, let's sum up our understanding of the conjunctions "although" and "though." Although these words are very similar, there are some differences in usage. Even though these words are very similar; there are some differences. These differences are very subtle, aren't they, though?

ANOTHER QUESTION

What's the difference between (d) *Even if* he comes, I won't see him, and (e) *Even though* he comes, I won't see him?

ANOTHER ANSWER

"Even if" means that a situation might occur and if that situation occurs the speaker will not engage in something. For example, I could say, "Even if I passed the entrance examination to that university I would not go there." So, we are speaking about what we would or would not do if something happened. In the case of (d) though we do not know if he will arrive, we know that if he does arrive, the speaker does not want to meet with him and will not meet with him.

"Even if" means the same as "whether or not" in common usage. In looking at the phrase "even though" the difference is that it means "despite the fact." With regard to (e), we sense the reality of his imminent arrival. He will come, and when he does, you will not see him. If we take "even if" and "even though" and use them in the following statements, you can see the difference with greater clarity:

> **(f) Even if I had a two-week vacation, I would not spend it at the beach this year.**
>
> **(g) Even though I have a two-week vacation, I'm not going to spend it at the beach this year.**

You can see that the first statement, (f), is speaking of a hypothetical situation, saying what the speaker would do if they had a two-week vacation, whereas (g) is dealing with an actual event. In (f) the speaker wonders what they would not do *if* they had a two-week vacation. In (g) the speaker has been given a two-week vacation and they are explaining that they will not spend the vacation at the beach this year.

Exercise 1

Match the sentence halves and make meaningful sentences.

1. She's quite intelligent,   (   )
2. Although he joined the company only six months ago,   (   )
3. Although I don't really enjoy watching boxing,   (   )
4. Whales are not fish but mammals,   (   )
5. He can play the violin,   (   )
6. She is very slim,   (   )
7. Although he worked very hard,   (   )
8. Although she is ninety-two years old,   (   )

    a. although most people think they are.
    b. although you might not think so.
    c. she is incredibly active.
    d. he's already been promoted.
    e. I did watch the title match.
    f. he was not able to pass the exam.
    g. although she eats like a horse.
    h. although he's not particularly good at it.

Exercise 2

Fill in the blanks so that each paired sentence will be synonymous.

1. Although it rained lightly, we went on a picnic.

   It rained lightly, (   ) we went on a picnic.

2. Although they have known one another for a long time, they're not good friends.

   (   ) (   ) (   ) (   ) (   ) that they
   have known one another for a long time, they're not good friends.

3. (   ) he is ninety-two years old, he is quite strong.

   He is ninety-two years old, but he is quite strong.

4. Although he gave her a good piece of advice, she didn't take it.

   He gave her a good piece of advice, but (   ) this, she didn't take it.

5. The park is rarely visited though it is very beautiful.

The park is rarely visited (　　　　　) (　　　　　) very beautiful.

Exercise 3

Complete the sentences using the words given in the square brackets.

1. Although [was, he, face, a, scared, he, death, put, to, on, brave].

   Although　　　　　　　　　　　　　　　　　　　　　　　　　　　　.

2. Even [by, is, Mr. White, is, though, teacher, strict, he, his, a, respected, students].

   Even　　　　　　　　　　　　　　　　　　　　　　　　　　　　　.

3. In [the, arrived, of, school, rain, spite, we, at, time, on, heavy].

   In　　　　　　　　　　　　　　　　　　　　　　　　　　　　　.

4. Even [if, not, speak, should, visit, French, Paris, does, I, she, she, think].

   Even　　　　　　　　　　　　　　　　　　　　　　　　　　　　　.

5. Young [seniors, he, is, he, though, better, his, than, knows].

   Young　　　　　　　　　　　　　　　　　　　　　　　　　　　　　.

6. I [gone, tell, not, he, her, knew, would, where, has, even, if, I].

   I　　　　　　　　　　　　　　　　　　　　　　　　　　　　　.

7. Even [solve, problem, couldn't, very, tried, hard, to, though, solve, the, he, he, it].

   Even　　　　　　　　　　　　　　　　　　　　　　　　　　　　　.

8. Although [is, father, Italian, Italy, he, from, doesn't, Nick's, speak].

   Although　　　　　　　　　　　　　　　　　　　　　　　　　　　　.

9. In [efforts, of, her, not, spite, she, her, could, goals, achieve].

   In　　　　　　　　　　　　　　　　　　　　　　　　　　　　　.

10. Despite [differences, together, are, their, they, well, getting, along].

    Despite　　　　　　　　　　　　　　　　　　　　　　　　　　　　.

Prepositions (part 1)

QUESTION

🎧 18

I learned in class that "among" is a preposition that denotes places like "between" which is used with words involving two entities, but "among" always introduces more than two entities. I believe this is true in many cases. But I came across a sentence like, "The old man divided three million dollars *between* [*among*] his two sons and a daughter" in an English grammar book where that rule does not seem to be followed. The book says that in this sentence, both "among" and "between" are allowable for use. But I think, according to the general rule, "between" could not be used because this word is employed with words which involve two entities. Could you explain what's going on in this particular case?

ANSWER

🎧 19

The simplest rule for the use of "between" and "among" is what you indicate. You can use "between" when you speak of two items, such as "Clio found her wallet *between* the sofa and the wall," or "Aya needed to choose *between* the chocolate and the vanilla cake for her party," and you use "among" when you speak of more than two items as in, "Aya needed to choose *among* several flavors for her cake" or "Jasmine felt lost *among* the crowd on the street," or "Pat was well known *among* the workers in the factory."

However, there is another set of circumstances that can help you decide which word, "among" or "between," should be used, and this is why you saw the use of the word "between" when the writer was speaking of three people in the sentence, "The old man divided three million dollars *between* his two sons and a daughter." The key is that the items, in this case, are distinct and known. We know that it was his two sons and his daughter that got the money, and because they are distinct and we can identify them, then we can use "between."

Think of it this way, if I can know exactly who got the money, then I can use "between." If I cannot be that exact, I would say, "The old man divided his money *among* his friends." Or, I could also say, "The old man divided his money *among* several charities." So, you can use "between" when the items under discussion are distinct, and "among" when they are not distinct. Let's look at some more examples to clarify this distinction.

If I said, "I try to divide my attention equally *between* my three children," the use of the word "between" is appropriate because you could recall and identify exactly who I divided my attention between: my three children. Also realize that there is nothing grammatically incorrect about saying "I try to divide my attention equally *among* my three children."

Another example that could be used is to say "Scott walked along the path *between* the trees," and we can do this because we are talking about specific sets of trees, one set on one side of the path and one set on the other. If I said, "Scott walked *among* the trees," there is no clear distinction about where the trees were located. Also, if there is a direct link between the items being discussed, you can use "between" for more than one item. For example, you could say that "There is some disagreement *between* the United States, Canada, and Mexico over the trade regulations." The central issue is the disagreement over "the trade regulations," and the author has provided the list of those countries that are in disagreement. If I was not going to be so exact, I would use "among," as in "There was disagreement *among* the countries regarding the trade agreement."

So, you see, there are some cases where *between* can be used when more than two items are being discussed. If the items are distinct, and individual, and can be identified after the statement is made, then you can use "between." If the items are not distinct, then you should use *among*.

between

among

Exercise 1

Choose the correct preposition.

1. The detective believes that there is no connection (between / among) the two murder cases.
2. The frightened dog began to run away with its tail (between / among) its legs.
3. The singer is very popular (between / among) young people.
4. She made two lifelong friends (between / among) her classmates at junior high school.
5. "Do you eat (between / among) meals or not?" the doctor asked me.
6. They are (between / among) the best baseball players in the United States.
7. Sally sat (between / among) her parents at the Christmas party.
8. I agree she is the best skier (between / among) us.
9. There are interesting similarities (between / among) the two cultures.
10. I eventually found the boy who stole my bag and ran away (between / among) the crowd of people.

Exercise 2

Complete the sentences with *at*, *in* or *on*.

1. I ran into George (   ) the bus stop this morning.
2. The lesson for today is (   ) page 35.
3. They may be swimming (   ) the pool now.
4. She gave the little boy a light kiss (   ) the cheek.
5. I found his name (   ) the top of the list of members.
6. A lot of stars are glittering (   ) the sky tonight.
7. I stopped at a convenience store (   ) the way home.
8. There's a Mr. Green (   ) the door asking for you, Jane.
9. Their two kids were (   ) the back of the car when they had the accident.
10. The Italian restaurant is situated (   ) the second floor.
11. We had to wait in a long line (   ) the hamburger shop.
12. After Sally and I had dinner, we had a drink (   ) the hotel lobby bar.
13. I noticed Marsha was wearing a diamond ring (   ) her finger.
14. Watch out! There's a hornets' nest (   ) the oak tree.
15. They drive (   ) the right in America, while we drive (   ) the left in Japan.
16. He enrolled in law school (   ) Columbia University.
17. You'd better write your name and address (   ) the back of the envelope.
18. A large television was (   ) the corner of the room.
19. John's house is (   ) the end of this alley.
20. He indicated (   ) the map how to get to the hotel.

Exercise 3

Complete the sentences with the prepositions given below.

[over, by, above, across, below, throughout, along, under, into, through]

1. There are two farms (   ) the river from the town.
2. He leaned (   ) the table and grasped my arm.
3. She loves strolling (   ) the streets of Paris.
4. I walked (   ) the front door and into the office.
5. The hotel is situated nearly 150 m (   ) the sea and you can enjoy impressive views from its lobby.
6. He fell down while skiing and broke his left leg (   ) the knee.
7. She kept her clothes, books, and other things (   ) the bed.
8. The jazz band performs (   ) the world.
9. She was standing (   ) the window, holding her baby.
10. A swallow flew (   ) the classroom through the window.

Exercise 4

Complete the sentences using the words given in the square brackets and then translate them into Japanese.

1. Needless to say, [recognized, medical, doctors, have, mind, close, long, the, that, there, is, relation, between, and, fact, body, a].

   Needless to say, _____.

   Japanese _____

2. His success [unexpected, friends, and, caused, entirely, was, surprise, his, among].

   His success _____.

   Japanese _____

3. Some [disadvantages, of, the, people, out, the, pointed, proposal], but on [I, the, am, for, whole, it].

   Some _____.

   Japanese _____

4. Why [issue, don't, when, mood, a, you, about, the, talk, boss, is, in, the, good]?

   Why _____?

   Japanese _____

5. There [corner, is, a, street, restaurant, nice, on, the, the, little, of, French].

   There _____.

   Japanese _____

Prepositions (part 2)

QUESTION

🎧20

I understand that both of the prepositions 'above' and 'over' mean "higher than." Therefore, for example, in a sentence like "John held an umbrella *above* [*over*] Yoko's head," both 'above' and 'over' can be used without making any substantial difference in meaning. But I think that as long as they are different prepositions, each preposition may have its own usage or usages. For example, how about the difference between (a) and (b) below?

> **(a) Ken's flat is somewhere above Jill's.**
> **(b) Ken's flat is somewhere over Jill's.**

I believe that (a) normally means that Ken's flat is situated on the third floor if Jill's flat is on the second floor and Ken's flat is "right above Jill's flat." In addition to this interpretation, is it possible to interpret this sentence to mean that Ken's flat is situated on the fourth or fifth floor which is not necessarily "just above Jill's flat," too? I mean is it possible to interpret this sentence to mean that Ken's flat may be situated anywhere as long as it is situated above Jill's flat.

On the other hand, (b) also means exactly the same as (a) does, in which Ken's flat is "just above Jill's flat." But with regard to (b), is there only the interpretation that Ken's flat is "vertically" right above Jill's flat even if it is on any floor? In other words, I would like to know whether or not Ken's flat must be interpreted to be situated exactly right above Jill's flat. Does (b) always mean that Ken's flat is just "right above" Jill's flat?

ANSWER

🎧21

The words *above* and *over* are used as adverbs, adjectives, and prepositions. As adverbs there is a difference in their meaning. As adjectives and prepositions, in most cases, they mean the same thing. So, as you use them as propositions in your questions, the words "over" and "above" are generally interchangeable; and, this is true in the two statements that you provide. Both (a) Ken's flat is somewhere above Jill's and (b) Ken's flat is somewhere over Jill's mean that you can find Ken's flat on a higher floor of the same building as Jill's flat. But, let's examine them carefully and see if we can find answers to your questions.

In response to your first question of (a) Ken's flat is somewhere above Jill's, the answer is that the nuance of the statement indicates that Ken's apartment could, indeed, be found anywhere on one of the upper floors of the building. It would be similar to me saying that there are storm clouds above the city. It does not mean that they are immediately atop the city, but that they are generally to be found within the airspace of the city and not simply hanging atop the tallest building, touching its uppermost floor. The nuance is fruitfully assisted by the adverb "somewhere" which indicates vicinity and not a specific location. As another example, I could say, "The house was in the mountains somewhere above the town." From this sentence, we know the generality of the location of the house, but not the specifics.

Regarding your second question, it actually has two dimensions. First you ask whether statements (a) and (b) can only be interpreted as meaning that Ken's flat is vertically right above Jill's flat. The answer is no, it does not indicate that the location is directly above Jill's flat. Instead, they both may be interpreted as meaning a general direction of being higher than Jill's in the same building. Again, the adverb, *somewhere* allows us to have this interpretation. If we remove the word "somewhere" from the statements, then the nuances can change.

If we say (a) Ken's flat is above Jill's, and (b) Ken's flat is over Jill's, the meanings then indicate a direct vertical association of Ken's and Jill's flats. In other words, we understand that both (a) and (b) mean Ken's apartment sits atop Jill's flat. It would be as if I said that "The sign is above the door," or "The sign is over the door." Each of these sentences naturally urges the reader or listener to look atop the door to find the sign. Likewise, this is the case with the circumstances of Ken's and Jill's flats. If you are on the street and looking at Ken and Jill's apartment building, and if someone says either Ken's flat is above Jill's or Ken's flat is over Jill's, then you need only find the window of Jill's flat and look up to the next window above to find Ken's flat.

above

over

Exercise 1

Complete the sentences with *above* or *over*.

1. The hotel is located (   ) the village.

2. The thief jumped (   ) the fence but was soon arrested.

3. His car plunged (   ) the bridge and into the waters of the river.

4. Her score on the math exam was way (   ) average.

5. She has, (   ) all, a wonderful personality, so everyone likes her.

6. He doesn't seem to have gotten (   ) the shock yet.

7. We saw the sun rising (   ) the horizon on the beach this morning.

8. The company sells various items all (   ) the world.

9. He ordered a pizza (   ) the phone.

10. This instruction book is on the shelf (   ) your head.

Exercise 2

Complete the sentences with the prepositions given below.

[off, up, inside, below, near, under, outside, behind, down, beyond]

1. The man has a deep cut (   ) his right eye.

2. He drank himself (   ) the table last night.

3. I heard her running (   ) the stairs.

4. They slowly walked (   ) the hill side by side, chatting amiably.

5. When I looked back, she was standing (   ) me, her arms folded.

6. As you can see, (   ) the mountain range there is a cloudless sky.

7. The family currently lives in Mount Vernon, (   ) New York City.

8. The carpenter fell (   ) the roof, but fortunately he was uninjured.

9. He stood (   ) the hotel entrance and waited for her.

10. I saw her put some expensive jewelry (   ) the box.

Exercise 3

Complete the sentences using the words given in the square brackets and then translate them into Japanese.

1. His [near, fifth, be, completion, "Love and Peace," book, is, titled, said, to].

   His _____.

   Japanese _____

2. He [the summit, to, about, and, below, 200 meters, rest, tired, down, sat, was].

   He _____.

   Japanese _____

3. They [the, hill, the car, and, into, down, drove, jumped].

   They _____.

   Japanese _____

4. The girl [the receptionist's, and, at, behind, me, desk, said, smiled, "Yes?"].

   The girl _____.

   Japanese _____

5. The view [beyond, from, spectacular, the mountain top, is, description, and].

   The view _____.

   Japanese _____

6. He suffered [by, off, from, to, for, his doctor, an illness, lay, was, and, a couple of months, alcohol, told].

   He suffered _____.

   Japanese _____

7. There [waterfall, river, further, is, the, a, up].

   There _____.

   Japanese _____

Unit 7 Prepositions (part 3)

QUESTION

I have noticed that a lot of Japanese students who are learning English confuse "by" and "until." I also must confess that I don't exactly know the correct usage of each word, either. The other day in our writing class, I translated " 私は7時までに家に帰らなければなりません " into "I have to go back home until seven o'clock," then I was told to use "by" instead of "until" in this sentence. And after I translated " 私は7時まで仕事をします " into "I will work by seven o'clock," I was told to use "until" and not "by" in this case. I would like to know how the words "by" and "until" should be used correctly. Could you give me your explanation?

ANSWER

🎧23

If you say "by" as in, "I must be home by seven o'clock," you must physically be in your home when the clock strikes seven o'clock. If you say, "I can stay out until seven o'clock," it means that you do not need to be in your home at seven o'clock, but merely finishing whatever you are doing outside at seven o'clock and then heading home. So, you can consider "by" to indicate a specific time when you have to finish something. It has something of an ultimatum in its connotation. For example, a teacher could say, "The test will start at 9:00 am and so you must be in the classroom by 8:50 am." If a teacher said this, it is an ultimatum, an order, or a command. In other words, the teacher is supposed to say "Be in the classroom by 8:50 am or you will suffer a bad fate." The word "by" can also be thought of as telling us when the last possible second that an action can be conducted. We could say, for example, that "I must be on the train by 9:00 pm." If you arrive at the train station at 9:01 pm, the implication is that the train left the station without you.

The word "until," on the other hand, is used to show the time period for an activity. For example, the sentence, "I will be playing baseball until six o'clock" gives us an indication of the time period of the practice or game. It shows the range of time that the activity or action will occupy. If I say, "I will study grammar from noon until midnight," it gives you the span of time during which I will undertake the activity of studying.

So, to summarize, "by" denotes a final time by which we must do something. The word "until" indicates a time frame during which we are going to be engaged in an activity or action. "By" is used to denote a stressful final point, and "until" is used to denote a relaxed sense of a period of time.

ANOTHER QUESTION

🎧24

It seems to me that both (a) and (b) have exactly the same meaning, but there must be some subtle difference between *on the morning of July 2* and *in the morning of July 2*. I would like to know your opinion or judgment about (a) and (b).

> **(a) We arrived in New York on the morning of July 2.**
>
> **(b) We arrived in New York in the morning of July 2.**

ANOTHER ANSWER

In the cases of (a) *We arrived in New York on the morning of July 2*, and (b) *We arrived in New York in the morning of July 2*, the first case, (a), is the more common expression. North Americans use "on the" to refer to a specific date when the arrival, or event, took place. In the case of (b), "in the" is usually used when we are referring to the time of day that the arrival, or event took place. North Americans would say, "I went to the park on Saturday morning," to give a specific time-frame for the trip to the park. They would also say, "I went to the park in the morning," to designate the time of day that they went to the park. Another example of this would be saying, "I left for the first day of class on the afternoon of September 1st," to designate the specific date and time of day that you made a specific journey. This is different from giving us the general time of day that you usually go to class by saying, "I leave for class in the afternoon."

However, the usage of either of the prepositions "on" or "in" would be contextually understandable to most English speakers. You are correct that they ((a) and (b)) *seem* to mean the same thing. But, there is actually a very small and subtle difference between them. The difference is one of emphasis. It is based on what the speaker wants to emphasize in the statement. In the case of (a) We arrived in New York on the morning of July 2, the speaker is emphasizing the time of their arrival in New York, which would be before noon. It's almost as though the speaker is substituting "on the morning" for a clock time, such as, 10:00 am. As another example, we could say, "I will purchase the tickets to the play *on the morning of August 7th*." In this case the speaker is emphasizing the time that the tickets will be purchased which will be before noon on that day. It's almost as though the speaker is substituting "on the morning" for a clock time.

In the case of (b), however, the emphasis is different. In (b) "We arrived in New York in the morning of July 2," the emphasis is on *the time of day* that the event (the arrival) took place, which was in the morning-time. Another example of this would be "The concert was held in the morning of September 5th." The emphasis is, likewise, the general time of day of the event, meaning whether it is in the morning, afternoon, or evening. This is a very subtle difference, and some might argue with our explanation, but if we are looking at very fine nuances, this is one interpretation that can be made to argue that there is a difference between the two phrases.

Exercise 1

Put in **by** or **until**.

1. I sent the letter yesterday, so it should arrive (   ) Friday.

2. He had to be at the airport (   ) nine thirty, but he couldn't arrive there because of the traffic jam.

3. The show ran (   ) November 27, 2022.

4. I guess I'll have to wait (   ) the right opportunity comes along.

5. Don't worry, kids. Your mom will be back (   ) noon.

6. It was dark (   ) the time he came back home.

7. She worked as a dancer and actress (   ) she was 80 years old.

8. He remained a very active musician (   ) he died.

9. The task is expected to be finished (   ) the end of this year.

10. She talked about her trip to France (   ) midnight.

Exercise 2

Complete the sentences with the prepositions given below.

[at, at, in, in, on, on, by, during, until, for]

1. She fell asleep (   ) the movie.

2. The dispute dragged on (   ) almost two years.

3. We'll be away (   ) July 24.

4. We'll be back (   ) July 24.

5. I'm meeting Mary (   ) lunchtime today.

6. George proposed to Sally (   ) her birthday and she accepted.

7. This restaurant has live music (   ) the evenings.

8. The meeting started at 3:00 p.m., exactly (   ) time.

9. The project of building this parking lot started (   ) the beginning of 2021.

10. At first John and Paul didn't get along very well, but (   ) the end they became good friends.

Exercise 3

Complete the sentences with the most appropriate phrases given in the square brackets below and translate them into Japanese.

> in time for dinner / at the end of the concert / during her youth / on time / in the past several years / by now / at sunset / for a long time / in about seven months / in the end / throughout the year / until midnight

1. She experienced several mysterious events (   ).

    Japanese _____

2. He was silent (   ) after he and his wife quarreled over a trivial thing.

    Japanese _____

3. He should have already arrived there (   ).

    Japanese _____

4. The bar is open (   ) Tuesday through Sunday.

    Japanese _____

5. The view of the sea was beautiful, especially (   ).

    Japanese _____

6. Her life has changed drastically (   ).

    Japanese _____

7. He wrote the novel (   ).

    Japanese _____

8. She was not able to come back home (   ) tonight.

    Japanese _____

9. Please be here (   ). Don't be late.

    Japanese _____

10. The band received, (   ), long applause and a standing ovation.

    Japanese _____

11. A lot of tourists visit the temple (   ).

    Japanese _____

12. The conductor asked her several times to become a regular member of his orchestra and, (   ), she accepted his offer.

    Japanese _____

Unit 8

Countable and Uncountable Nouns

QUESTION

🎧 26

In our English grammar class, I had a lesson about "Countable Nouns" and "Uncountable Nouns." But I am confused with respect to the distinction between them, because our teacher said in class that "water" is an uncountable noun; therefore, it is impossible to count it like "one water" or "two waters." But when I was reading a novel, I came across an expression like "The waters were rising." The word "water" is normally said to be an uncountable noun, but it seems to be treated as a countable noun in the novel. Moreover, I found an expression like "Two coffees, please," in another book. This expression seems to be used in everyday conversation. So how can we explain the example "The waters were rising," and "Two coffees, please."?

I have also come across expressions such as "He gave me a talk on economics," and "That's crazy talk," where the former sentence has a countable noun (i.e. a talk), while the latter has an uncountable noun (i.e. talk). Could you tell me what exactly countable and uncountable nouns are and how we should distinguish between them?

ANSWER

🎧 27

A countable noun can be tallied, or added up. For example, I could put a number in front of a countable noun: one cat, two cats, three cats, four cats, etc. Uncountable nouns cannot be calculated, summed, or tallied. As you know, countable nouns are those that can actually be counted, and they have both a singular and plural form. For example, "There was a car parked in the driveway," uses a singular form of the countable noun "car." "I saw three purple cars on the highway today," uses the plural form of the countable noun "car." Countable nouns can have an "a," "an," or "the" in front of them and can have a singular or plural form. So, if you simply think, when encountering a noun, whether it can be physically counted, you can usually safely judge whether it is countable or uncountable. You will find that most nouns are countable nouns.

Uncountable nouns are those that would usually be simply impossible to count. They are also known as "mass nouns" or as "non-countable nouns." These nouns cannot be made plural. You cannot simply put an "-s" at the end of an uncountable noun and make it plural. You would not use "a," or "an." In other words, you could not say "a rain." You could use "any" or "much" with uncountable nouns. You could ask, for example, "Has there been any rain in the countryside?" There are many uncountable nouns. A short list of them would include such words as *advice, coffee, knowledge, news, sand, sugar, traffic,* and *water.* But, be careful, sometimes an uncountable noun can seem countable if it is joined by a countable noun in a phrase. For example, we could say, "Let me give you a piece of advice." It seems, then, that advice becomes countable, but it is actually the word "piece" that is being counted. Likewise, we could say, "I looked at a grain of sand under the microscope." Again, it seems that sand is now countable, but in reality, the word "grain" is what is being counted. What is adding to the confusion is that some uncountable nouns, such as "coffee" can be countable under certain situations. For example, I could go into a coffee shop and order "two coffees." In this case, we are actually envisioning "cups of coffee," but idiomatically speaking, the use of "cups" isn't necessary, because an English speaker would understand what was meant from the situation. The hearer would think, "I am in a coffee shop, my friend has ordered two coffees, and he is actually asking the server to bring two cups of coffee to our table."

The phrases that you refer to, "The waters were rising," and "He gave me a talk on economics" may be confusing, but if you think of water as coming from different locations in an area that is flooding, it makes sense that a plural form is used. For example, let's say a huge rain storm is causing the river near my house to rise and flood, and likewise the rain is causing a pond near my property to overflow, and also a lake near my property to rise and flood its shoreline. In a case like this, we could say that the river water, the pond water, and the lake water are all rising; hence, we choose the plural usage.

In the case of the "He gave me a talk on economics," we could envision a professor of business being asked by one student to explain, or give a talk, about economics, and another student wanting information about regional commerce, and another student asking about international trade. Each "talk" is separate and about a separate topic. It's like going to a coffee shop and ordering a cup of coffee, a cup of hot chocolate, and a cup of tea. Hence, we choose the usage of the singular.

Exercise 1

Choose the correct words to complete the sentences below.

1. I went fishing and caught more than five (fish / fishes) today.
2. She showered and changed (cloth / clothes) and then went out.
3. While traveling we should watch our (belonging / belongings) at all times.
4. There are many (sheep / sheeps) and horses on the farm.
5. Please accept my (thank / thanks) for your wonderful present.
6. I saw a girl running up the (stair / stairs) instead of taking an elevator.
7. He earned a lot of (money / moneys), saved it, and bought a luxury car.
8. He put down his (baggage / baggages) at the gate, held her tight, and kissed her good-bye.
9. How many (deer / deers) are there in the nature park?
10. The village had no (electricity / electricities) eight years ago.

Exercise 2

Put in the most appropriate word in each bracket from the list below to complete the sentences below. [luggage, furniture, patience, advice, hair, permission, knowledge, damage, information, progress]

1. I would like to hear some (   ) about how to deal with a situation like this.
2. She lives in an old Victorian house filled with antique (   ) in San Francisco.
3. The earthquake caused a lot of (   ) to the city.
4. Kazuko is making good (   ) with her English.
5. You need to get (   ) from the author before quoting the passage.
6. The article gives (   ) on the problem of global warming.
7. She doesn't have much (   ) about that matter.
8. She had long (   ) when she was a college student.
9. How much (   ) am I allowed to take with me?
10. I really appreciate your (   ) and cooperation.

Exercise 3

Choose the correct one.

1. He gave me (two informations / two pieces of information) about the event.
2. Could you give me (some advice / some advices) on how to lose weight?
3. The little boy had (eggs / egg) on his cheek.
4. I guess I'm catching a cold. I feel chilly and have (a sore throat / sore throat).
5. I hope I will have (a nice weather / nice weather) when I get there.
6. He says he loves what he is doing, but I know it is actually (hard works / hard work).
7. I would like (some ice / some ices) in my drink.
8. I think you should consult your lawyer before making (a decision / decision).

Exercise 4

Complete the sentences with the words given in the square brackets and translate them into Japanese.

1. He [years, as, of, has, experience, doctor, twenty, a].

    He _____.

    Japanese _____

2. My [my, are, on, overseas, formed, experiences, views, through, things, largely].

    My _____.

    Japanese _____

3. It [that, of, information, a, the, is, source, good, Internet, true], but it sometimes gives us unreliable information.

    It _____,

    but it sometimes gives us unreliable information _____.

    Japanese _____

4. If [enjoy, recommend, that, well, you, to, plan, I, you, want, travel, really, definitely].

    If _____.

    Japanese _____

5. This [cleaner, space, to, light, vacuum, little, and, is, takes, carry, up].

    This _____.

    Japanese _____

Exercise 5

Translate the following English words into Japanese.

1. glass   (   )
2. a glass   (   )
3. iron   (   )
4. an iron   (   )
5. paper   (   )
6. a paper   (   )
7. room   (   )
8. manner   (   )
9. manners   (   )
10. custom   (   )
11. customs   (   )

Formal and Informal Expressions

QUESTION

🎧 28

It seems that every language on earth has "formal" and "informal" expressions. In the case of English, I learned that, for example, the following (a) and (c) are "formal" sentences, while the following (b) and (d) are "informal" ones.

> **(a) The meeting was postponed until next week.**
> **(b) The meeting was put off till next week.**
> **(c) The police are investigating the case now.**
> **(d) The police are looking into the case now.**

What exactly do you mean when you say, "formal English" and "informal English"? And could you give me other contrastive expressions that clearly distinguish between "formal English" and "informal English"?

ANSWER

🎧 29

Formal language often means that it follows prescribed rules and is appropriate for business settings or occasions of ceremony, such as at a wedding or funeral. We use formal language when we speak with a superior, or someone important. If you go to a job interview, for example, you would use formal English.

Casual language, or informal English, is language used when one is in a relaxed environment. Often a person will use casual English with his or her friends or siblings, for example. It is English that is used outside of business and when you are not at an important ceremony. It is English that you would use if you had a conversation with a group of friends. Let me give some examples of Formal and Casual (or Informal) English to illustrate the differences.

Let's say that you are inviting a business associate out to lunch to discuss an upcoming business deal, you might say, (A) "Mr. Richardson, I would like to invite you to lunch on Tuesday to discuss the upcoming company merger. Are you available on Tuesday afternoon at 12:30?" Now, if you were inviting a friend out to lunch next Tuesday, you might ask him or her in this fashion: (B) "Hey Jodie, what are you doing next Tuesday around noon? Do you want to get together for lunch?" Notice that in the formal example (A) we used the individual's family name as opposed to (B) where we used the first name. Also, in (A) there was a specific question "Are you available on Tuesday afternoon at 12:30?" after the specific topic was identified. The sentence "I would like to invite you to lunch on Tuesday to discuss the upcoming company merger," would naturally follow. In (A) Mr. Richardson was given the information about what specifically was being addressed upfront; however, in (B) the friend opened the discussion with a question, "Hey Jodie, what are you doing next Tuesday around noon?" This would not be acceptable in a formal setting.

Also, using the examples you provided, we can see other differences. In Formal English the speaker or writer avoids using idiomatic expressions, favoring instead concrete words that are harder to misinterpret. This is especially important in business, as you want to be understood completely by those with whom you are doing business. So, let's examine the first set of examples:

> **(a) The meeting was postponed until next week.**
> **(b) The meeting was put off till next week.**

The formal sentence (a) uses the word "postponed" whereas the informal English sentence (b) uses the idiomatic expression "put off" instead. In the second set of sentences ((c) and (d)) the same pattern occurs and the formal English sentence uses the word "investigating" whereas the informal sentence uses the idiomatic expression "looking into" instead. Lastly, I would like to add that in many cases a single verb tends to be used as a formal word and a phrasal verb as an informal one.

Exercise 1

Which expression is formal or informal? Write (**F**) if it is formal and write (**I**) if it is informal.

1. You might want to consider changing your plan.   (   )
    You'd better change your plan.   (   )
2. Neither of us agree with the plan.   (   )
    Neither of us agrees with the plan.   (   )
3. In which country do you hope to live?   (   )
    Which country do you hope to live in?   (   )
4. The boy needs friends with whom he can play.   (   )
    The boy needs friends to play with.   (   )
5. It's me who loves you.   (   )
    It is I who love you.   (   )
6. What kind of music are you interested in?   (   )
    In what kind of music are you interested?   (   )

Exercise 2

Which sounds more polite or softer, (a) or (b)?

1. (a) I hope you can give me some advice.
    (b) I'm hoping you can give me some advice.   (   )
2. (a) I was wondering if I could invite you to dinner next Friday?
    (b) Is it all right for me to invite you to dinner next Friday?   (   )
3. (a) I would be most grateful if you could help me with my work.
    (b) I will be most grateful if you can help me with my work.   (   )
4. (a) I can lend you $100.
    (b) You can borrow $100 from me.   (   )
5. (a) Her behavior was sort of rude.
    (b) Her behavior was rude.   (   )

Exercise 3

Fill in the round brackets in order to make the second sentences sound more formal or polite using the words given in the square brackets. [**get, get, an, kind, please, apologies, would, of, speak, honor, hear, may, if, about, might, wonder, truly, allow, back, express, mind**]

1. Can you give me a ride to the station?
    I was wondering (   ) you could (   ) give me a
    ride to the station.
2. May I open the door?
    (   ) you (   ) my opening the door?
3. Thank you for taking time to see me.
    It was very (   ) (   ) you to take time to see me.

4. Is Marsha there? [on the phone]
   (   ) I (   ) with Marsha, please?
5. I'm sorry for your father's passing.
   I was sorry to (   ) (   ) your father's passing.
6. Nice to meet you.
   It's (   ) (   ) (   ) to meet you.
7. I need your answer as soon as possible.
   Could you (   ) (   ) to me with an answer as soon as possible, please?
8. This is on me.
   Please (   ) me to (   ) this.
9. I'm really sorry.
   I'd like to (   ) my sincerest (   ).
10. Could you tell me how to operate the copying machine?
    I (   ) if you (   ) be able to tell me how to operate the copying machine.

Exercise 4

Choose the informal counterparts from the expressions given below.

come across / find out / get out / call for / think over / put up with / Thanks / fix / hide / ask / build / get / What? / break in / call off / take in / deal with

formal	informal
I am grateful to you.	( )
I beg your pardon?	( )
cancel	( )
conceal	( )
consider	( )
construct	( )
deceive	( )
demand	( )
discover	( )
enquire	( )
escape	( )
find	( )
handle	( )
interrupt	( )
purchase	( )
repair	( )
tolerate	( )

Unit 10
Expressions Referring to "Future Time"

QUESTION

 30

In English there are several expressions that refer to "future time." Since there are several expressions that we can use to talk about the future, I'm not sure which expression is suitable in which contexts or situations. For example, I came up with the following five sentences to talk about the same future event:

> **(a) I will see her tomorrow.**
> **(b) I'm going to see her tomorrow.**
> **(c) I see her tomorrow.**
> **(d) I'll be seeing her tomorrow.**
> **(e) I am to see her tomorrow.**

Before I got into college, I had thought all the above sentences meant precisely the same thing. But now I think that all the sentences are subtly different in meaning, and I would like to know the exact differences that exist among the above sentences. Could you tell me which expressions should be used in which contexts or situations?

ANSWER

30

The five choices do mean *essentially* the same thing. Each lets us know that you will meet with a woman tomorrow. However, as you indicate, there are differences. One difference is in the setting in which each may appropriately be used. Some are more formal, and others are more informal. Also, statement (e) indicates that the speaker might not have been the one to schedule the meeting. Let's look at each one in turn.

Regarding (a) "I will see her tomorrow," the speaker or writer is being formal. Perhaps he or she is responding to a question from his or her employer asking the question, "When will you meet with our new client?" To respond "I will see her tomorrow," displays a certainty and shows that the speaker or writer is in control of the situation. When one says, "I will," it shows determination and confidence.

In the case of (b) "I'm going to see her tomorrow," it is a bit more casual, and indicates confidence that the meeting will take place. It would not be out of bounds for a reply in a casual business setting if, let's say, a coworker stops you in the hallway and enquires, "Will you be meeting with the new client this week?" You can reply "I'm going to see her tomorrow." It is a notch less formal than (a) but still alright for general business settings. In regard to (c) "I see her tomorrow," it is a confident statement, but it is rather curt, or short and to the point. It would not be appropriate to say to one's employer, but might be said to friends or family.

Examining (d), "I'll be seeing her tomorrow," this is a casual statement that would be alright in a setting with friends. Since the comment has a contraction, it can be seen to be more casual. So, the phrase, "be seeing her," is not business English.

Finally, when we look at statement (e) "I am to see her tomorrow," it is as if the appointment has been set for the speaker or writer and not by the speaker or writer. For example, we could imagine the following situation. Perhaps the speaker or writer has gotten into trouble at university, and he or she has been called in to see the Dean of Students. In such a case, he or she would respond to a question regarding the appointment by saying, "I am to see her tomorrow."

It seems that this type of expression (be to + infinitive) is also used in newspaper or magazine articles as a formal expression as in, for example, "The US president is to visit Japan to see the Japanese Prime Minister next month."

Exercise 1

Complete the sentences with **will ('ll)** or **(be) going to**.

1. **A:** I can't go shopping today.
    B: Then, I (   ) go shopping for you.

2. It's getting very cloudy. We (   ) have rain soon.

3. I definitely recommend this movie. I'm sure you (   ) enjoy it.

4. **A:** Has anybody offered to prepare supper?
    B: George (   ) do it.

5. **A:** Did you buy tickets for the concert?
    B: No, I forgot. I (   ) book them as soon as possible.

Exercise 2

Choose the appropriate expression.

1. John (looks after / will look after) my dog while I'm away next weekend.
2. Take an umbrella in case it (rains / will rain).
3. Let's go on a picnic if the weather (is fine / will be fine) tomorrow.
4. The musical (starts / is starting) at 6:30pm according to the program.
5. "Just a moment. I (am going to / will) show you my new dress," said Meg.
6. What (are you doing / do you do) this afternoon?
7. I'll call you when I (get there / will get there).
8. I'm sorry I can't come to your party. I (will flying / am flying) to London tonight.
9. I've got to go now. I (will call you back / 'm going to call you back) later.
10. I think it's (raining / going to rain) before long.

Exercise 3

Change the following sentences into grammatical ones.

1. I promise I never leave you alone again.

    _____

2. The sky has clouded over. It rains.
    The sky has clouded over. _____

3. You must finish your homework before you will go out.

    _____

4. At this time tomorrow they are swimming in the park's lake.

    _____

5. I send you the pictures if you like.

_____

6. I see him tomorrow, so I'll say "Hello" to him for you.

_____

7. When you will see Kate, tell her I'm getting along very well.

_____

8. You will never pass the examination unless you will study harder.

_____

9. As soon as I will arrive in San Francisco, I'll get in touch with you.

_____

10. Next Saturday at this time I will have dinner with Kate.

_____

Exercise 4

Underline the correct form.

1. Be careful with the vase. It (breaks / will break) easily.

2. She's pregnant. She (is going to / will) have a baby.

3. We ('re playing / will play) baseball this afternoon. Would you like to play, too?

4. **A:** This black bag costs $500, but the brown one is a little cheaper.

   B: Well, (I'm going to take / I'll take) the brown one then.

5. **A:** Have you decided yet?

   B: Yes, I ('ll have / have) the sirloin steak, please.

6. The conference (is going to begin / begins) next Saturday afternoon at 14:00.

7. **A:** Can I talk to you for a minute?

   B: Sorry, (I'm just leaving / I'm just going to leave).

8. We (are giving / will give) a birthday party for John on Friday evening and we'd like you to come.

9. **A:** What are your plans for tonight?

   B: We (will see / are going to see) a movie. We bought the advance tickets on the Internet three days ago.

10. I seem to have lost my passport. What (will I do / am I going to do)?

Expressions of Reason and Cause

QUESTION

🎧32

There are some phrases such as "due to," "because of" and "owing to" that express "reason" and "cause." But I don't know when and how these phrases are used properly. For example, the contents of "Tom is successful due to his efforts," could also be expressed as "Tom is successful because of his efforts," and "Tom is successful owing to his efforts." So, I would like to know the appropriate usage of these three phrases and the subtle meaning differences among them.

ANSWER

🎧33

"Due to," "because of," and "owing to," are so similar that, in almost all cases, there would be no confusion if you interchange them. However, there are some subtle differences in meaning, or, at least, some debates over some possible differences in nuance between the three. Let me explain.

Let's first identify the grammatical points of these phrases. "Due to" is mostly used as a complex preposition, as is the phrase "owing to." However, some old English teachers might insist that the word "due" in the phrase "due to" should only be used as an adjective. If this is the case, a person using the phrase "due to" would have to say, "The success of the player was due to his determination to win." In this example, the adjective "due" modifies "to his determination to win." However, this insistence that "due" be used as only an adjective is contested, and textbooks and dictionaries that have been published over the past decade all seem to be okay with "due to" being used as a complex preposition.

As is well known, the phrase "owing to" is synonymous with "because of." We would use the phrases "owing to" and "because of" in sentences such as "Owing to your hard work, you received a passing grade in the English class," and "Because of the scholarship the young couple was able to quit their jobs and go back to university." In the case of "due to" we would use it in a sentence such as "The plane's delay was due to bad weather." If you think all of these sentences sound too similar to be different, you won't be too far from the truth. In everyday usage the phrases "due to," "because of," and "owing to," are similar enough that they can usually be used interchangeably without any confusion about meaning. Then what are the differences between these three phrases? I think we can find stylistic differences between them. First of all, the phrase "due to" is mainly used in America and this phrase is used in both formal and informal situations, so this phrase could be found in everyday conversations as well as in journalistic publications and even literary works. The phrase "because of" is used as a colloquial expression, so this phrase can be heard in everyday conversations. Regarding "owing to," this phrase is found both in British and American English, and in my view this expression seems to be widely employed both formally and informally. Incidentally, the phrases "on account of" and "attributable to" are also synonymous with the three phrases, but these phrases seem to be found, usually, only in very formal sentences.

ANOTHER QUESTION

There are conjunctions which refer to reason or cause: *as*, *because* and *since*. Could you describe the basic differences among the three words in brief?

ANOTHER ANSWER

These conjunctions, *as*, *because*, and *since*, are used to introduce subordinate clauses, clauses that cannot stand alone. The conjunctions "as" and "since" emphasize the result of an action, as "because" does, by introducing the reason for what occurred or what will happen in the future. The conjunction "as" may be used to make a statement such as, "As my daughter was the highest scorer in the preseason intermural scrimmages, the coach chose her for the varsity soccer team." The rationale, the reason, is given, in the case of "as" at the beginning of the sentence. Likewise, "since" follows the same pattern: Since my daughter was the highest scorer in the preseason intermural scrimmages, the coach chose her for the varsity soccer team. So, what is the difference between "as" and "since"? The answer is where they fall on the formality scale. "Since" is more formal than "as." Except for this, they are interchangeable. One thing to point out is that we will usually place a comma after the clause introduced by "as" or "since." Note that that was what was done in the sentence previously introduced, "Since my daughter was the highest scorer in the preseason intermural scrimmages, (comma) the coach chose her for the varsity soccer team.

The conjunction "because" implies a rationality or reason that something occurred. It often occurs after a main clause; however, there is no problem with placing "because" at the beginning of a sentence, though that sounds more declaratory than explanatory. For example, although I could say "The coach put my daughter on the varsity soccer team because she was the highest scorer in the preseason intermural scrimmages," I could also say, "Because my daughter was the highest scorer in the preseason intermural scrimmages, the coach put her on the varsity soccer team." This is perfectly fine, but it sounds like you are arguing a point in a court of law. So, please understand that one can, successfully, change the location of "because" to be at the beginning of a sentence. But this does not always mean that this usage will sound stilted and declaratory in every situation. That is to say, there are also cases where this conjunction is used as a word that simply denotes a reason or cause even if it is put at the beginning of a sentence. In any case, *because* is more commonly used than *as* or *since*, so it also has the benefit of being more familiar sounding and in a real way, friendlier.

Exercise 1

Match the sentence halves and make meaningful sentences.

1. I think this philosophy book is important ( )
2. A great number of animals are said to have gone extinct ( )
3. As it was getting dark, ( )
4. Since I only had a small amount of money, ( )
5. Owing to poor health, ( )
6. The disappearance of the glacier on the mountain was ( )
7. Because I have a severe headache, ( )
8. She was fortunate ( )
9. The game was postponed ( )
10. Her life has completely changed ( )

    a. I bought a cheap used car.
    b. because it explains how to lead a meaningful life.
    c. thanks to his help.
    d. he was exempted from military service.
    e. I won't be able to go to the party.
    f. I started walking faster to the mountain hut.
    g. in that she was able to find the right doctor in the right hospital.
    h. due to global warming.
    i. because of habitat loss.
    k. on account of bad weather.

Exercise 2

Complete the sentences by using the words given in the square brackets.

1. They [was, the game, to, cancel, hard, as, it, decided, raining, very].

    They   .

2. I [I, the office, felt, hours, so, left, quite, two, early, exhausted].

    I   .

3. As [was, took, the shade, it, very hot, a while, we, a rest, in, getting, for].

    As   .

4. I [I, my work, on, concentrate, my attention, because, felt, couldn't, sleepy].

    I   .

5. Since [to, up, on, you're, making, French, Paris, you, should, brush, an official trip, your].

    Since   .

6. Thanks [to, information, can, large, amount, the Internet, we, easily, get, a, of].

    Thanks   .

7. The car [account, dense, occurred, accident, was, have, to, on, of, the, reported, fog].

    The car   .

8. John [illness, unable, the conference, was, to, because, attend, of].

    John   .

9. We [change, were, budget, to, the project, obliged, due, to, cuts].

    We   .

10. Owing [caused, areas, torrential, to, many, the storm's, movement, rains, flooding, in, slow].

    Owing   .

"If ... not" and "Unless"

QUESTION

🎧 36

I understand that "If the weather is not fine, the game will be canceled" can replace "Unless the weather is fine, the game will be canceled" or "John never helps you with your job if you don't ask him to do so" can replace "John never helps you with your job unless you ask him to do so." As can be seen in these sentences, "if ... not" can replace "unless," but I would like to know exactly which expression is used in what situations, since there must be subtle meaning difference between "if ... not" and "unless." So, could you tell me how to use each expression properly?

ANSWER

🎧 37

You are correct that the conditional "unless" generally has the same meaning as the conditional phrase "if ... not." There are many examples in which "unless" and "if ... not" can be interchanged. As the following examples show, they can be interchanged while maintaining almost the same meaning: "*Unless* you exercise, you will not pass the physical education examination," and "*If* you do *not* exercise, you will not pass the physical education examination," or "*Unless* you change your mind, nothing will change," and "*If* you do*n't* change your mind, nothing will change."

So, the word, "unless" and the phrase "if ... not" may usually be interchanged. However, there are cases where the two expressions cannot be interchanged and this reminds us of "the one form—one meaning principle" that was advocated by the famous American linguist Dwight Bolinger. Take the following sentence as an example: *If the state had not increased taxes, there would not have been so many angry citizens.* Of course, this sentence is perfectly grammatical. On the other hand, simply using "unless" will make the sentence ungrammatical. That is to say, we cannot say, "Unless the state had increased taxes, there would not have been so many angry citizens." Likewise, we could not substitute "unless" for "if ... not" in this statement, "If the football coach had not selected Sam to play, there would not have been so many goals scored." I mean we would not be able to successfully maintain the meaning of the original statement if we said "Unless the football coach selected Sam to play, there would not have been so many goals scored." To further help you understand, let me offer an additional example where "unless" is not a good substitute for the "if ... not."

You could use "if ... not" in this sentence: "If the student had not studied harder, he would have failed his English class." However, we can't successfully make an exchange of *if ... not* with *unless*. It would not make sense to write the sentence "Unless the student had studied harder, he would have failed his English class." In this way, we cannot generally use "unless" to refer to "unreal" situations in this construction. One reason for this is that the use of "unless" does not usually work in the case where the subjunctive mood is used.

In most cases, as explained, you are fine interchanging *if ... not* with *unless*. However, in some cases, especially in those involving the subjunctive mood as shown above, exchanging *unless* for *if ... not* is awkward and does not adequately convey the meaning of the sentence.

Now let me explain about "unless" and "if ... not" in more detail below. As we have seen above, there are cases in which "unless" and "if ... not" are interchangeable but there are also occasions when it is impossible to use one in place of the other. Let's look at other cases where we cannot exchange "unless" for "if ... not." "Unless" cannot replace "if ... not" in a sentence like "I'll be surprised if the Tigers does not win." We usually use "unless" to say that something can only happen or be true in particular circumstances. In other words, "unless" means "except on the condition that" or "except if." That is the reason why we cannot say "I'll be surprised unless the Tigers wins." because with regard to this sentence we can assume that there are plural factors that satisfy the condition of the main clause. I mean the reason why "I'll be surprised" is not limited to "the Tigers' not winning" but to other cases, too.

In cases where the main clause is an interrogative sentence, not "unless" but "if ... not" should be used as in "What should I do if I don't get the green light from the boss?" In place of this sentence, we couldn't say "What should I do unless I get the green light from the boss?"

Lastly, let me explain the difference between the following pair.

> **(a) If the president does not meet our demands, we will go on strike.**
>
> **(b) Unless the president meets our demands, we will go on strike.**

It is true that both of them convey the same meaning, but "unless" is said to be stronger than "if ... not," so sentence (b) would be more preferable and appropriate as an ultimatum.

Exercise 1

Match the sentence halves and create meaningful sentences.

1. Nothing changes ( )
2. She won't tell you about herself ( )
3. He couldn't know the fact ( )
4. Nowadays, no one can travel internationally ( )
5. He'll leave the company ( )

    a. unless she told him.
    b. unless you change your mind.
    c. unless you can persuade him otherwise.
    d. unless you ask her to do so.
    e. unless they are very rich.

Exercise 2

Choose the appropriate expression.

1. (Unless it rains tomorrow / Unless it will not rain tomorrow), I'll go cycling up the hill.

2. I'll be surprised (if they don't get married / unless they get married).

3. (If you don't pass the math exam / Unless you pass the math exam), what will you do?

4. I would go for a walk (if I didn't have this lower-back pain / unless I had this lower-back pain).

5. She'll come to the party if she is free – (unless her parents stop her / if her parents don't stop her).

Exercise 3

Complete the sentences using the words given in the square brackets and then translate them into Japanese.

1. I [caught, the last, have, train, couldn't] if I [not, thirty minutes, left, had, earlier].

   __I_____if I_____.__

   Japanese _____

2. He'll [persuade, otherwise, go, I, there, can, him, unless].

   __He'll_____.__

   Japanese _____

3. Satiated bears [they, humans, provoked, severely, rarely, unless, attack, are].

   __Satiated bears_____.__

   Japanese _____

4. He [unless, questions, asked, seldom, speak, I, would, him].

   __He_____.__

   Japanese _____

5. We [to, walk, the station, unless, can, it's, raining, in which case, to, take, we'll, have, a bus].

   __We_____.__

   Japanese _____

Causative Verbs

QUESTION

🎧38

In high school we learn the verbs "let" and "make" are used to denote similar meaning and take the same sentence patterns, as in (a) "John let me go there alone" and (b) "John made me go there alone. "But, when the sentences are translated into Japanese, both of the sentences can be translated with exactly the same Japanese expression, which actually causes students confusion. When I got into college, I came to know that there is some difference between sentences such as (a) and (b). But I can't clearly tell (a) types from (b) types, so would you please give me an explanation about "let" and "make"? In addition, I would like to know other similar expressions like (c) "John had me go there alone" and (d) "John got me to go there alone." When and how exactly do we use these four types of sentences?

> **(a) John let me go there alone.**
> **(b) John made me go there alone.**
> **(c) John had me go there alone.**
> **(d) John got me to go there alone.**

ANSWER

🎧39

The difference between "let" and "make" is based on the willingness of the person being asked or required to do something and also who initiated the activity. If you say, as in sentence (a), "John let me go there alone," it tells us that you asked John to allow you to go someplace alone, and John said yes. From this sentence, we could, for instance, imagine a situation in which John is your older brother and has been given responsibility for you, and you asked him to allow you to go someplace alone and he agreed. This is when you would use the sentence "John let me go there alone." We could also say, "My parents let me travel to Tokyo on the train alone," and this would imply that you asked your parents for permission to go to Tokyo on a train alone. You initiated the request.

With regard to the statement (b) "John made me go there alone," the implication is that John ordered you to go someplace alone. John initiated the decision and did so in a manner that denotes that he is your superior, or, at least, in charge of you in some way. We could also have a sentence such as, "My teacher made me complete the project alone," and this would imply that the teacher initiated the action (by assigning the project) and then controlled the circumstances by making (ordering, requiring, directing) that you complete the project by yourself. On the other hand, sentence (a), "John let me go there alone," as mentioned above, implies that you wanted to go somewhere by yourself and you asked John for permission, and he permitted you.

Sentence (b), "John made me go there alone," means that John ordered you to go someplace alone. John controlled the circumstances, with the implication being that he told you to go alone (which might not be something you wanted, whereas in sentence (a) it implies that you got what you wanted).

Let's move on to the final part of your question. You asked what the difference was between "(c)John had me go there alone," and "(d)John got me to go there alone." Well, the issues are power and control. In (c) the implication is that John had power and control over you. So, the sentence tells us that you had no choice but to go there alone. In (d) we do not know if John compelled you, but the sentence at least implies that he had to talk you into doing what he wanted you to do.

In conclusion let me summarize the meaning of each of the sentences

(a) John let me go there alone.

This statement shows us that John exercises power over the speaker. The speaker has, evidently, asked for permission from John to go, and John has granted that permission. In any case, clearly, the speaker wanted to go to somewhere alone.

(b) John made me go there alone.

This statement indicates, as with (a) that John exercises control over the speaker; however, it does not indicate that the speaker wanted to go to the location but was possibly ordered to do so alone. Statement (b) seems to indicate a bit of tension, or even anger about the fact that John made the speaker go there alone.

(c) John had me go there alone.

This statement, like the last two above, indicates that John has control over the speaker. Yet, it is gentler in tone than statement (b). Sentence (c) indicates that John wanted the speaker to go to the location alone, but it sounds like it was not so much a direct order as a request.

(d) John got me to go there alone.

This statement does not indicate that John ordered the speaker to go someplace, but that the speaker acceded to a request for a favor by John. Unlike the other statements, we do not really know if John ordered the speaker to go to the location, but we do know that John wanted the speaker to go somewhere alone and asked him or her to do so.

Exercise 1

Fill in the blanks with the most appropriate words given below.

[get, got, makes, made, made, let, let, let, had, had]

1. Against my will, he (   ) me drink many glasses of wine.
2. Her parents won't (   ) her travel abroad by herself.
3. The boss (   ) his secretary spruce up his office.
4. His wife (   ) him to stop drinking.
5. Love (   ) the world go around.
6. Please (   ) me know if you have a problem.
7. I (   ) my brother wash the car.
8. We'll have to (   ) the doctor to come and see our two-year-old son.
9. The ending of the movie (   ) me very happy.
10. (   ) me explain about the matter a little more.

Exercise 2

Complete the sentences using the words given in the square brackets and then translate them into Japanese.

1. The mere [made, being, the little girl, thought, of, left, alone, nervous].

   The mere _____ .

   Japanese _____

2. In case [sister, I'll, you, out, need, help, have, my, help, you].

   In case _____ .

   Japanese _____

3. If you think [our, you're, we're, to, let, very, much, daughter, walk, alone, to, school, going, mistaken].

   If you think _____ .

   Japanese _____

4. How [has, to, to, do, I, him, realize, the matter, he, nothing, worry, regarding, get, about]?

   How _____ ?

   Japanese _____

Exercise 3

Match the sentence halves to complete meaningful sentences.

1. His warm words of comfort　　　　　(　)
2. He hopes he will have someone help him　　(　)
3. I let her guess　　　　　　　　　　(　)
4. We're trying to find a way　　　　　(　)

      a. to get our sick mother to see a doctor.
      b. before I told her the correct answer.
      c. to find a nice apartment suitable to his needs.
      d. made her feel closer to him.

Exercise 4

Translate the following sentences into Japanese.

1. The school authorities are investigating what caused the school building to be burned by the fire.

Japanese _____

_____

2. A mild heart attack forced him to stop his research for a while.

Japanese _____

3. His words made me smile and his attitude made me feel very good.

Japanese _____

Middle Constructions

QUESTION

🎧40

I sometimes come across such expressions as "This car drives smoothly," "The book sells like hot cakes," or "The movie is showing now." Before I got into college, I had not seen or heard sentences like these. I came to know these types of sentences are called "middle constructions" or "activo-passives" in my English grammar class in college. Could you tell me the characteristics of this type of sentence and in what situation this kind of sentence is used? Grammatically speaking, this type of sentence is strange because the subject in the middle construction plays functionally an object role and not a subject role but the subject noun phrase functions as if it were the subject. I would like to know why this weird type of sentence exists in English.

ANSWER

🎧41

This car drives smoothly, the book sells like hot cakes, the movie is showing now – all of these sentences sound like they could be found in an advertisement. "These sentences are called "middle constructions" and you can hear them when you watch television advertisements or when you listen to radio commercials. Here are some more examples of middle constructions, "This video camera records clearly" "This motorcycle rides comfortably" and "This tent folds up easily after use." This type of construction has been given several names over time. They are also known as "activo-passive constructions" or "derived intransitive constructions." So, it is no wonder you are confused. I will adopt the term "the middle construction" below because a great number of researchers employ this term nowadays.

It would perhaps be helpful for us to review the main characteristics of the middle construction. They can be summarized in the following four points:

❶ The middle construction is used to show the characteristics or nature of the subject noun in a sentence.

❷ In the middle construction the verb form is usually in the simple present tense, though it may also be used in the past tense (i.e., This car sold well).

❸ Manner adverbs or adjectives are normally used in the middle construction, but be aware that occasionally they do not appear in this construction at all (i.e., This dress buttons, but that dress zips).

❹ In the middle construction the object noun of a transitive verb is placed at the subject position.

Now that we have reviewed the main characteristics of the middle construction, let us remind ourselves that English, like most languages, evolved, borrowing various elements such as words, phrases and constructions from other languages. The middle construction is said to have derived from Latin which is the parent of the modern Romance languages like French, Italian, Spanish, and Portuguese. And Latin is originally from what is termed a *proto-Indo-European* language. So, the origin of the middle construction goes back several thousand years, well before English became the English we know today.

The middle construction is most commonly used when the speaker or author wants to express how an action can or cannot be carried out when he or she uses or deals with something as a tool or with something which has some function. For instance, if you want to say that a garden watering hose can be put away easily you could say it in this manner: "When no longer needed, the hose rolls up easily." Or if you were commenting on an author's style of writing, you could say this, "Dickens language, once considered natural and unaffected, now reads as old fashioned."

With regard to the sentence "This car drives smoothly," it tells us that although the agent (the driver) actually drives the car, it gives us the impression that the car runs as if it drove by itself smoothly with no effort by the agent. As for the sentence "The book sells like hot cakes," it tells us that, with no labor of the agent (the book seller), he or she can sell the book because of the excellent contents or some other good characteristic of the book. Whenever you want to express how easily, comfortable, quickly, efficiently, or otherwise an action can be accomplished without your effort, then you can use the middle construction. I will end with a middle construction: This answer reads well! (I hope).

Exercise 1

Fill in the blanks with the most appropriate verb given below and translate them into Japanese. **[keep, sells, paints, waxes, spreads, pull out, eats, cuts, photographs, plays]**

1. This piano (   ) easily.

   Japanese _____

2. Fish doesn't (   ) well, not even in a fridge.

   Japanese _____

3. Mary (   ) well.

   Japanese _____

4. This meat (   ) well.

   Japanese _____

5. This pumpkin (   ) well.

   Japanese _____

6. These weeds (   ) easily.

   Japanese _____

7. Softened butter (   ) easily.

   Japanese _____

8. The fence (   ) easily.

   Japanese _____

9. This car (   ) well.

   Japanese _____

10. This floor (   ) easily.

    Japanese _____

Exercise 2

Complete the sentences using the words given in the square brackets and translate them into Japanese.

1. This [Teflon, easily, pan, cleans, frying].

    This _____.

    Japanese _____

2. This [easily vacuum, anywhere, cleaner, stores].

    This _____.

    Japanese _____

3. This [it, if, cooks, all, slow, the, meat, better, you, cook].

    This _____.

    Japanese _____

4. This [time, item, at, sells, year, well, this, of].

    This _____.

    Japanese _____

5. On [the, paper, whole, well, this, reads].

    On _____.

    Japanese _____

Exercise 3

Explain the differences between (a) and (b) sentences below in Japanese.

1. (a) He doesn't photograph well. / (b) He is not good at photography.

    _____

    _____

2. (a) The shirt irons well. / (b) The shirt was ironed well.

    _____

    _____

3. (a) This car will sell easily. / (b) This car will be sold easily.

    _____

    _____

Negative Expressions

QUESTION

Compared to the Japanese language, there are many more negative words in English. So, as a consequence, perhaps there are many negative expressions in English. The problem is that sometimes various negative expressions in English look similar and it is difficult to find subtle differences in meaning among them. In other words, I sometimes find it hard to tell similar negative expressions apart. For example, I would like to know the difference in meaning between the following two expressions, (a) and (b).

> **(a) She's not a singer.**
> **(b) She's no singer.**

Also, could you tell me the differences in meaning between (c) and (d) as well as (e) and (f)?

> **(c) She's not a fool.**
> **(d) She's no fool.**
> **(e) Many students don't like the singer.**
> **(f) Not many students like the singer.**

ANSWER

Let's start with your first question. You asked about the difference in meaning between (a) "She's not a singer," and (b) "She's no singer." Well, the first case, (a) "She's not a singer," can be a statement of fact. The speaker or writer might just be pointing out the reality that the person who is being spoken or written about is not a singer. It could also be interpreted as saying that the person is a bad singer. However, this would only be clear depending on the context in which the statement is used. If I said, for example, "My goodness, that was awful, she's not a singer," I would be saying that she is a bad singer. However, if I asked, "We need to add people to our rock and roll band, how about having Suzie be the lead singer?," someone could respond, "She's not a singer, she's a drummer." In that case, there is no malice or hurt intended in the comment.

Now, the circumstances are different for the second statement, (b) She's no singer. In the case of "She's no singer," the speaker or writer is making a critical statement about the person's ability to sing. It would be just like the person being criticized had sung in front of a group of people, and the speaker or writer was criticizing her singing ability. By saying, "She's no singer," a person is saying that the singer cannot sing well. It could be taken as a mean, or highly critical comment, and, if heard or read by the singer, would be taken as an insult. It would be as if I saw a baseball player drop a ball during a game and then said, "He's no baseball player," I would be saying that he is not a good baseball player.

In the case of (c) She's not a fool and (d) She's no fool, the difference is not so stark or clear. The first example, "She's not a fool," is a statement of opinion given in reflection about the person's abilities. It would be as if I were thinking of an employee's performance and said, "He's not a problem." It isn't a passionate statement, only an observation. However, the phrase, "She's no fool," is more of a passionate statement about someone, and the speaker comes across as appreciating, or liking, the individual. I could also say of someone who fooled a scam artist who was trying to steal his money that "He's no fool." I am implying a sense of admiration for the person, and am saying that he is too intelligent to fall for the scam artist's tricks.

In the case of (e) "Many students don't like the singer," and (f) "Not many students like the singer," the difference might be understood if we think of percentages. If I say that "Many students don't like the singer," I am not saying that a majority of students do not like the singer (over 50%). I am simply saying, that a large number of students, but probably less than 50%, do not like the singer. I could also say, "Many students don't like eating in the cafeteria." In this case also, the number is not over 50%, but still sizeable (e.g. 48% or 49%). If I say "Not many students like the singer," I am implying that most students do not like the singer, or that the number of those who do not like the singer is over 50%. It would be as if I was saying "Not many students like homework." This would also imply a number over 50%. Also, notice that in the example (e) "Many students don't like the singer," the negative "not" negates the verb "like" and the whole sentence is a negative sentence, while in the example of (f) "Not many students like the singer," the negative "not" negates the quantifier "many" and the whole sentence is an affirmative sentence. That is to say, the (e) and (f) sentences differ in that the former simply denotes that the number of those who do not like the singer is sizable but not over 50%, whereas the latter focuses on the number of those who like the singer and indicates that that number is low (e.g. less than 50%). But either way the statements let us know that the singer is not popular.

Exercise 1

Complete the following sentences with the words given in the square brackets below and then translate them into Japanese. **[nothing, nowhere, no, nobody, none, any]**

1. There is (   ) doubt about his innocence.

   Japanese _____

2. It's (   ) of your business who I date.

   Japanese _____

3. I can't work with him (   ) more.

   Japanese _____

4. (   ) knows for sure where Jane has gone.

   Japanese _____

5. There is (   ) like cold beer after work.

   Japanese _____

6. Jane is (   ) to be found.

   Japanese _____

Exercise 2

Choose the right words.

1. The math exam was very tough. (Nobody / Anybody) could pass it.
2. There's (no one / anyone else) I really want to come with me apart from you.
3. I don't know (nothing / anything) about the matter.
4. I don't have (any / no) money with me. Can you loan me 10 dollars?
5. They didn't do (nothing / anything) over the weekend.

Exercise 3

Fill in the blanks so that each pair of sentences will have almost the same meaning.

1. Both Sally and Kate dislike snakes.
   (   ) Sally (   ) Kate like snakes.

2. Every rule has some exception.
   There is (   ) rule (   ) some exceptions.

3. They are really music lovers. Whenever they meet, they always talk about music.

   They are really music lovers. They (   ) meet (   ) talking about music.

4. There wasn't any explanation as to why the accident happened.

   There (   ) (   ) explanation as to why the accident happened.

5. His ability to solve the problem is anything but certain.

   His ability to solve the problem is (   ) (   ) certain.

6. I have never played lacrosse.

   I (   ) (   ) played lacrosse.

7. The building is no longer in his possession.

   The building is (   ) in his possession any (   ).

Exercise 4

Translate the following sentences into Japanese.

1. He is by no means a lazy person.

   Japanese _____

2. She loves movies but she seldom watches horror movies.

   Japanese _____

3. Being rich does not always mean being happy.

   Japanese _____

4. She would be the last person to say such a thing.

   Japanese _____

5. Not every person can be a professional soccer player.

   Japanese _____

6. All of the students didn't pass the exam.

   Japanese _____

7. None of the students passed the exam.

   Japanese _____

8. In her life, his mother was never free from care.

   Japanese _____

Passive Constructions

QUESTION

We learn in school that a passive sentence is made from an active sentence. For example, "The cup was broken by the little boy," is made from "The little boy broke the cup." Thus, in order to get a passive sentence, the pattern [X + a transitive verb + Y] is transformed into the pattern [X + be + a past participle + by + X]. We learn that this is the rule when we make a passive sentence. Probably in many cases, this "rule" works when a passive sentence is produced, but in other cases this rule obviously does not work. For example, it is impossible to make a passive sentence from a sentence like "I have two sisters," or "He resembles his father." If we apply this rule to the sentences, we get such sentences as "Two sisters are had by me," or "His father is resembled by him," which are obviously ungrammatical and unacceptable. So, I would like to know the true rule when a passive sentence is produced. Would you please tell me what condition(s) may be involved in making passive sentences?

Additionally, I have another question. As is well known, there are two types of "passive sentences" i.e., "be" passive sentences and "get" passive sentences. For example, there are two kinds of expressions like (a) and (b) below. Could you please tell me the difference between the pair of sentences below, as well?

> **(a) Sally was fired.**
> **(b) Sally got fired.**
> **(c) Mike was injured.**
> **(d) Mike got injured.**

ANSWER

As we know, a passive sentence is a sentence in which the subject (which is originally the object in an active sentence before passivization) is interpreted to get the action done to it and is placed in the subject position as the focus or theme of the sentence. For example, a letter gets written, but it does not write itself and a car gets fixed, but it does not fix itself, etc.

Basically, the subject of a passive sentence is not doing the action, but having the action done unto it, as can be seen in a sentence such as "The painting is being painted by Pablo." When we make a passive sentence from an active sentence, the receiving object in the active sentence is placed at the beginning of the passive sentence, and, as a result, the object of the active sentence and the subject of the passive sentence switch positions. For example, instead of saying "Shakespeare wrote the play," we would say,

"The play was written by Shakespeare."

We could also change the active sentence "Pat wrote the book," to the passive "The book was written by Pat." Therefore, to make a passive sentence, basically, the format [the object of an active sentence + be + a past particle + by + the subject of an active sentence] is adopted. In fact, in many cases, we can make passive sentences according to this format or rule. But why doesn't the rule work all the time? Why is "I have two sisters" not able to be magically changed into a correct and grammatical passive?

Well, let's examine our rule again. There are three things that help us identify a sentence as a passive sentence. First, if the subject in the sentence is interpreted not to be doing the action, the sentence is passive. Second, the verb in the sentence is always a form of be + a past participle. Third, it is common for the entity doing the action in the sentence to be introduced by the preposition "by," as in "The house was built by Babe Ruth." So, why does all of this not work with your two examples, "I have two sisters," and "He resembles his father?" Did the subject create his or her two sisters? Did the subject create the resemblance between himself and his father? Was there an action done in either of these sentences? No, no action is expressed in either sentence. For a sentence to be passive, it must usually contain an action of some sort and your examples do not. That is one fundamental reason that the Action to Passive voice structural change does not work successfully. To add another example, you cannot successfully change, "Herman belongs to a football team," to "A football team is belonged to by Herman," because, in reality, there is no action. No action = no active sentence; no active sentence = no chance of a passive sentence.

In your second question, you wanted to know the difference between the "be" passives and the "get" passives. In the case of poor Sally, when you say, "Sally was fired," it indicates that her job ended, but perhaps not through her fault. If you say, "Sally got fired," it indicates, or hints very strongly, that Sally did something to get herself fired. For example, you could expand "Sally was fired" by saying "Sally was fired due to downsizing at her company." That would work and would make Sally a sympathetic character. You could expand, "Sally got fired" by saying "Sally got fired because she argued with her boss," Likewise, in the case of unfortunate Mike, in the example, "Mike was injured," it sounds like Mike could have been injured by someone else, but in the case of "Mike got injured," it sounds like he was up to something and hurt himself as a result. So the distinction between the "be" passive and the "get" passive is based on how much responsibility the subject bears for what happened to him or her.

Exercise 1

Rewrite the following sentences with passive forms.

1. They speak English in New Zealand.

   _____

2. The police are still investigating the robbery case.

   _____

3. The government might impose an additional tax on fossil fuels.

   _____

4. They established the state university in 1868.

   _____

5. Kenji explained the situation to me.

   _____

6. The strong winds blew down a great number of trees.

   _____

7. The company has built a new building in front of the station.

   _____

8. James painted the fence green.

   _____

9. The nurse is taking care of the old woman.

   _____

10. They say that he will be promoted to general manager.

    _____

11. Who broke the vase?

    _____

12. Kate was given a diamond ring by Tom.

    _____

13. Everyone in his family laughed at him.

    _____

14. People looked up to him as a role model.

    _____

15. His brother told him to pull himself together.

    _____

Exercise 2

Complete the sentences using the words given in the square brackets.

1. She [after, named, grandmother, Margaret, was, her].

   She _____.

2. He [one, pianists, considered, to, of, best, in, is, the, be, the world].

   He _____.

3. The [injured, in, treated, seriously, man, is, the, emergency, being, room].

   The _____.

4. That [all, as, man, them, is, honest, known, of, an, to, person].

   That _____.

5. Kate [German, lesson, being, given, a, is, by, a, musician, piano] now.

   Kate _____ **now**.

6. The drunken man [car, got, got, run, injured, over, by, a, and, seriously].

   The drunken man _____.

7. He [was, exercise, advised, to, more, by, his, get, doctor].

   He _____.

8. The [will, the, demolition, by, of, completed, building, be, Christmas].

   The _____.

9. I've [treated, had, of, being, like, a, enough, kid].

   I've _____.

10. I hear [phones, Japan, were, the, cell, cameras, sold, with, first, in].

    I hear _____.

Exercise 3

Fill in the blanks so that each pair sentence will mean almost the same.

1. George Martin donated the collection to the museum in 2022.
   The collection (   ) (   ) to the museum by George Martin in 2022.
2. They will have finished the job by next week.
   The job will have (   ) (   ) by next week.
3. They took no notice of her.
   No notice was (   ) (   ) her.
4. It is said that Margaret is a great pianist.
   Margaret is said (   ) (   ) a great pianist.

Present Perfect Forms

QUESTION

🎧 46

I would like to know the difference in meaning between (a) and (b) below. Although I consulted some English grammar books, I couldn't find the difference in meaning between the present perfect form and the present perfect progressive form seen in the following pair of sentences:

> **(a) He has played the violin since he was five years old.**
>
> **(b) He has been playing the violin since he was five years old.**

I have another question. Our teacher said in our English grammar class that some researchers regard the following type of sentence as being odd or ungrammatical because the sentence contains the present perfect form.

> **(c) Einstein has visited Princeton University.**

But I think this sentence could be improved to be good or grammatical by adding some word or phrase to it. If I am right, what kind of expression is needed to make the sentence acceptable? Regarding (c), please note that I am talking about the physicist Albert Einstein (1879-1955) who is famous for his theory of relativity.

ANSWER

🎧 47

Let's start with your questions regarding (a) He has played the violin since he was five years old, and (b) He has been playing the violin since he was five years old. As you mention, (a) is an example of the present perfect form, and (b) is that of the present perfect progressive form, respectively. What is the present perfect form? Basically, the present perfect form is used to express past actions or activities that are relevant to or continue into the present. With regard to (a), it is an expression of an action happening in the past, and it focuses on when that action started and also implies that the past action is related to the present. On the other hand, the example (b) which is in the present perfect progressive form also functions just like the example (a) with the present perfect form does, but it is different from (a) in that it puts emphasis on the duration of the action that the subject has been performing.

As another example of the present perfect form, I could give "My friend Ahmed has surfed since he was fourteen years old." This sentence focuses on the general time frame when the action of the subject started and also denotes that the subject is still engaging in the action at the present time, too. And as additional examples of the present perfect progressive form, you could say, "My friend, Bob, has been playing tennis since he was twenty-one years old," or "I've been studying Spanish since I was in college." Each of these statements not only indicates that the activity that the subject started in the past has been continuing up to the present but also emphasizes the "sense of the continuity" of the activity.

So, to sum up the answer to your first question, sentence (a) He has played the violin since he was five years old, is different from sentence (b) He has been playing the violin since he was five years old, in that (a) emphasizes when the action started while (b) gives special importance to the duration, or how long it has been going on.

Regarding sentence (c) Einstein has visited Princeton University, it would actually work as a response to a question, such as, "Has Einstein ever visited Princeton University?" or "Has Einstein ever visited an American university?" However, as a stand-alone sentence, without the introduction of a question/response matrix, I would recommend rephrasing it as *Einstein has been to Princeton University in the past.* or simply, *Einstein has visited Princeton University in the past.* The use of the phrase "in the past" keeps each sentence from being, and sounding, too abrupt or unclear.

ANOTHER QUESTION

I guess that Einstein is not alive at the present time, therefore it is odd to say something about his present situation, which might be the reason why (c) *Einstein has visited Princeton University* sounds odd. But if we add an adverb like "even," would (c) be improved and be acceptable? I mean would "*Even Einstein has visited Princeton University*" be all right?

ANOTHER ANSWER

It would only be correct if you said "Even Einstein visited Princeton University." If you say *Even Einstein has visited Princeton University*, the implication is that Einstein is still alive. As "has visited" is a present perfect and therefore denotes a time frame that is not yet over. As Einstein is dead, it would be impossible for him to visit Princeton University at present.

Exercise 1

Based on the situations given in the first sentences, complete the sentences with the present perfect, using the verbs, *be*, *forget*, *disappear*, *lose*, and *improve*.

1. His suitcase was here, but it isn't here anymore.

   His suitcase _____ .

2. Bob is looking for his watch. He can't find it.

   Bob _____ .

3. She told me her e-mail address, but I can't remember it now.

   I _____ .

4. Keiko's French wasn't very good. But it is better now.

   Keiko's French _____ .

5. She came to the office at 9:00 and now it's 14:00.

   She _____ **in the office for five hours** .

Exercise 2

Change the verbs in the round brackets into the appropriate forms and then translate the completed sentences into Japanese.

1. She (know) Mr. Jones for more than twelve years. ( )

   Japanese _____

2. I (be) to Paris three times. ( )

   Japanese _____

3. My grandfather (be) dead for three years. ( )

   Japanese _____

4. It (be raining) off and on since last night. ( )

   Japanese _____

5. I want to know what (become) of her since that time. ( )

   Japanese _____

6. She's always (be) good to me. ( )

   Japanese _____

7. This is the most wonderful story I (ever hear) in my life. ( )

   Japanese _____

8. I (save) about $1,000 so far. ( )

   Japanese _____

9. He says he (never see) a ghost in his life. (   )

Japanese _____

10. A Mr. Green (wait) for you for some time. (   )

Japanese _____

11. It took a lot longer than I (expect) to finish the task. (   )

Japanese _____

12. I think I (finish) the task by the end of this week. (   )

Japanese _____

13. Next month he (live) in this city for eight years. (   )

Japanese _____

14. By the time I got to the airport, the plane (already leave). (   )

Japanese _____

15. I (wait) for Jane since noon, but she doesn't show up. (   )

Japanese _____

Exercise 3

Complete the sentences using the words given in the square brackets.

1. I [I, have, computer, years, seventeen, used, the, since, was, old].

    I _____.

2. She [been, piano, over, has, three, playing, the, for, hours].

    She _____.

3. He [attend, had, conference, that, he, decided, would, already, the].

    He _____.

4. It [went, since, has, three, years, the, been, man, missing].

    It _____.

5. No [wife, burst, than, had, he, that, laughing, his, out, sooner, said].

    No _____.

6. How [you, been, for, the, long, working, company, have]?

    How _____?

7. In [married, will, years, been, for, have, twelve, they, June].

    In _____.

8. She [is, the, have, most, ever, person, I, talented, met].

    She _____.

Possessive Constructions

QUESTION

🎧 50

There are two methods to indicate "possession" in English: that is to say, "X's Y" and "the Y of X." For example, you have "Tom's decision" and "the decision of Tom" "Sally's mother" and "the mother of Sally" or "the dog's tail" and "the tail of the dog" and so on. In these cases, it is possible to transform "X's Y" into "the Y of X" or vice versa. But it seems that this kind of transformation does not always work properly because a grammar book I read mentions that it is completely possible to say, for example, "John's landlord," but if you say "the landlord of John," it may sound strange or awkward. So, my question is the following: Under what condition(s) are the use of "X's Y" or the use of "the Y of X" permitted? Also, I would like to know the difference(s) between the former method (X's Y) and the latter method (the Y of X) of showing possession. My question might sound cumbersome, but could you give me your explanation about the two possessive constructions, please?

ANSWER

🎧 51

You are right that this is a tough question to answer, but if we break it down into its parts we can get a clearer understanding. In most cases, the difference is one of casualness versus formality. In the case of where we would use the structure of "X's Y" such as the statement "Hiro's toothbrush," we employ it as a more casual expression than "the toothbrush of Hiro" which has the structure of the Y of X.

Now, let's examine the difference between the use of "X's Y" and that of "the Y of X" in detail below. For instance, when you respond to a question from a friend who asked "Whose bicycle is that?" you can respond simply, "Mie's bicycle," or more thoroughly, "That's Mie's bicycle." This "X's Y' pattern is the normal, colloquial form of the statement of possession. It is the most common, and can be used in most settings with friends and also in more formal business settings, and even in situations with strangers. Among friends you can say, "Alex's book," "Ayako's glasses," or "Alice's café." You can also use it in common settings outside your circle of friends, as when you are asked by your teacher, "Whose brilliant English homework is this?" and you can respond, "It is Kenji's homework." Notice that we include "It is" or "That's" as we saw in "That's Mie's bicycle" above as additional elements of each sentence. This elongation of the sentences makes them sound polite.

The "Y of X" format is less common, and is, in reality, rather rare. To say, "That is the car of Robert" sounds archaic, and we get the impression that the sentence is the expression that someone would say in a Shakespearean play or in a very old English novel. However, as a matter of fact, even now these types of possessive expressions can be used correctively. For example, if I were to respond to the question, "Whose child is this?" I could respond, "That is the son of Bob." This would be alright and would not sound too out of place.

Likewise, I could respond to the question, "Whose cat is that?" by saying, "That is the cat of Pat." Again, it would not be used as commonly as saying "That's Pat's cat," but it would be used from time to time. As already mentioned above, the difference is that one is more a formal expression than the other. That is to say, "X's Y" is less formal than "the Y of X." We could also say, "That boat belongs to Jasmine," or "That hat belongs to Clio." This is more common a structure than "That is the boat of Jasmine," or "That is the hat of Clio." So, there are other structures to denote possession than the X's Y and the Y of X structures.

There seems to be a tendency that in the X's Y construction, X is typically an animate noun, especially a human noun, while in the Y of X construction, Y is typically an inanimate noun. For example, using the X's Y construction, we might say, "That's Clair's hat," "That's Angie's car," or "That's Farmer Brown's cow." On the other hand, using the Y of X construction, we could say, "That's the hat of Clair," "That's the car of Angie," or "That is the cow of Farmer Brown." While the Y of X construction is a bit old fashioned sounding, as the above examples show, you can still find examples of it being used.

Lastly, let's consider the expression "Tom's book." This expression may be interpreted to be equivalent to "the book belonging to Tom," "the book written by Tom," "the book Tom is reading," or "the book Tom published," and so on. In this way, "Tom's book" can be interpreted in a number of ways. How about an expression like "the wheel of the car?" This expression can be interpreted to denote the "part-whole" relation (i.e., the wheel (part) and the car (the whole)). So, in a nutshell, the structures of X's Y and the Y of X may be used to denote not only "possession" but other kinds of relationships between X and Y. For that reason, it would considerably be difficult to fully understand the nature of these two types of constructions. But it seems that a key to interpreting what meaning these two constructions express may greatly depend on our understanding of the context, scene, or our knowledge of the real world.

Exercise 1

Rewrite each phrase using the possessive apostrophe.

1. the daughter of Mr. Brown   _____

2. the pen that belongs to Peter   _____

3. the cars that belong to Ted and Meg   _____

4. the speech of the politician   _____

5. the works of the artist   _____

Exercise 2

Make the following sentences grammatically correct.

1. That's the cellphone of Pat.

   ⇒ _____

2. John was finally able to place the flag on the mountain's top.

   ⇒ _____

3. The bank is on the street's corner.

   ⇒ _____

4. The experiment's results were interesting.

   ⇒ _____

5. The fossil dinosaur's discovery put the town on the map.

   ⇒ _____

6. Have you seen the new car of Tom?

   ⇒ _____

7. I like his tie's color very much.

   ⇒ _____

8. It goes without saying that some heavy smokers develop lung's disease.

   ⇒ _____

9. When the musician was young, his mother gave him music's lessons.

   ⇒ _____

10. It was great fun climbing to the scraper's top.

    ⇒ _____

11. I borrowed the book of Mary yesterday.

⇒ _____

Exercise 3

Which is the right expression in the usual circumstances? Put the answer in the round bracket.

1. (a) Mary's bag / (b) the bag of Mary: (   )
2. (a) Sally's eyes / (b) the eyes of Sally: (   )
3. (a) Paul's landlord / (b) the landlord of Paul: (   )
4. (a) the house's windows / (b) the windows of the house: (   )
5. (a) the living's cost / (b) the cost of living: (   )

Exercise 4

Make the following two sentences one sentence containing the apostrophe s ('s).

1. It was a very interesting lecture. It was yesterday.

   _____

2. John sent me a letter. It encouraged me to carry on the research.

   _____

3. My grandmother had an operation. It was successful.

   _____

4. Jim Young has published a new book. It is selling like crazy.

   _____

5. Tom and Kate own a shop. It's around the corner.

   _____

Exercise 5

Consider the interpretations of the following expressions and translate them into Japanese.

1. George's book   _____

2. a painting of Ann's   _____

3. a painting of Ann   _____

Existential Sentences

QUESTION

There are at least two ways to introduce the existence of an entity or entities in English. For example, you have the following two types of existential sentences or existentials:

> **(a) There are three windows in this room.**
> **(b) This room has three windows.**
> **or**
> **(c) There are five pockets in this jacket.**
> **(d) This jacket has five pockets.**

My question is: When and how do you distinguish the *there*-existentials like (a) and (c) and *have*-existentials like (b) and (d)? In other words, under what principles or rules are these two constructions employed respectively?

ANSWER

First, we should establish what is meant by "existential" sentences. These are special sentences that use an unusual sentence construction. Essentially, they denote the existence of an entity (a thing or a person).

As you have noticed, in your examples (a) and (c) that the word "there" is used. The "there" in an existential sentence has no specific meaning like the adverb "there," so it is called an "expletive." The term "expletive" is often assumed to be simply a curse word, but, in this case, it is not a curse word. It is helpful because it plays a role as the subject of a sentence. For example, using the expletive "there" as subject will allow the writer or speaker to put the real subject in the focal position in the sentence and have the reader or listener pay attention to the existence of the real subject. As we saw above, there are two distinct purposes when an expletive "there" is used as a subject. We will examine first how a speaker can use "there" to show the existence of a subject before it is introduced into a discourse. Let me explain with a bit more detail, as some may find this to be complicated.

Please understand that the existential *there* construction may be used to introduce the existence of a new entity or entities into the discourse. By using the expletive "there" as a "dummy subject" in this construction, it is possible to delay the real subject's entrance into the sentence and the focal point is put on the real subject and consequently its existence stands out and is emphasized. Perhaps it could be said that it elevates the drama of the subject's introduction. Why is it called a "dummy subject" you might ask? Basically, because it has no substantial meaning on its own and is used only to add special emphasis to the ensuing real subject. So, to reiterate, the basic function of the existential *there* construction is to introduce the existence of an entity or entities into the discourse.

Let's look at the examples (a) *There are three windows in this room* and (c) *There are five pockets in this jacket.* The emphasis is put, in the case of (a) on the *three windows* and in (c) on that of *five pockets.* We could also create such sentences as "There are five good players on the team" or "There is a single goldfish in the pond." In each case the words being emphasized are located in the middle of the sentence and the reader or listener is encouraged by the construct to pay close attention to the numbers (all of the examples from you and me involve numbers and if you look at the construction carefully, you will find that it often involves noun phrases with numbers).

Then, how is this construction different from the *have*-existentials? Specifically, the difference between your examples of the *there*-existentials (a) and (c) and the *have*-existentials in the case of (b) and (d) offer some interesting observations. In the first pair (a) *There are three windows in this room* and (b) *This room has three windows* there is a difference of emphasis or focus. In (a) what is being emphasized or focused, or what the reader or listener notices, is the "three windows." The mental image first gravitates to the concept of the three windows. In (b) the emphasis or focal point is put on the room. The first image is of a room, then the three windows are added to the mental image of the room. Likewise, in (c) *There are five pockets in this jacket* and (d) *This jacket has five pockets,* the emphasis or focus in the case of (c) is put on the five pockets, and in (d) on the jacket.

This brings us to your questions: *When and how do you distinguish the there-existentials and have-existentials? In other words, in what principles or rules are these two constructions employed respectively?* The key is within the decisions of the author or speaker. What does he or she want to have the reader or listener pay attention to? Does he or she want to emphasize what is in or on something? Does he or she want to emphasize the existence of the windows or the room or does he or she want to emphasize the pockets or the jacket? If you want to emphasize the smaller item included on or in the larger item, then use the there-existential and if you want to emphasize the larger item in which the smaller item resides or is on, then use the have-existential construction. For example, I could decide to emphasize the number of chairs in a room by saying, "There are five chairs in the room." The reader or listener's attention is directed to the chairs. Or, I could thematize the room by saying "The room has five chairs." The reader or listener's attention is then turned to the room. So, it is up to the author or speaker to decide where to place the emphasis and then select the existential structure to allow that emphasis to be made.

In sum, in (a) and (c), the writer or speaker presents the existence of "three windows" and "five pockets" to the reader or listener for the first time and the very existence of them is indicated as the most important, whereas in (b) and (d), the characteristics of "this room" and "this jacket" are mentioned as the primary concern of the writer or speaker.

Exercise 1

Correct any errors found in the following statements. Note that two of the following six statements do not have any errors.

1. There's the personal computer on the desk.

2. A mistake is in the report.

3. Your breakfast is on the table.

4. A loud noise was from the cellar.

5. Something wrong is with the copy machine.

6. The pen is on the table.

Exercise 2

Write new sentences with similar meanings beginning with "there."

1. It seems that there were misunderstandings between the couple about the matter.

   There _____.

2. It happened that there were some guests at my home last night.

   There _____.

3. As there was no evidence of fraud, the suspect was released.

   There _____.

4. It appears that there has been some improvement in relations between them.

   There _____.

5. There was no objection, so his request for funding was granted.

   There _____.

Exercise 3

Choose the correct ones.

1. (a) There is a stranger at the door.
   (b) The door has a stranger at it.   (   )
2. (a) There is a girl in the yard.
   (b) The yard has a girl in it.   (   )
3. (a) The tree has a nest.
   (b) The tree has a nest in it.   (   )
4. (a) There is a cat on the stairs.
   (b) The stairs has a cat on it.   (   )

Exercise 4

Match the sentence halves and make meaningful sentences.

1. There is a good reason   (   )
2. There was a wealthy woman   (   )
3. There was never any doubt   (   )
4. There are various kinds of   (   )
5. There are few students in the class   (   )
6. There are still many unanswered questions   (   )

a. problems that we have to solve.
b. who understand the difference between formal and informal English.
c. about the origin of the Japanese language.
d. why she turned down his offer.
e. in my mind about his ability to perform the task.
f. at the party whose husband ran a big company.

Unit 20 Simple Forms of Verbs and Progressive Forms of Verbs

QUESTION

🎧 54

It is said in English grammar books that the so-called "stative verbs" cannot be allowed to occur in the progressive form. I understand that for example, verbs like 'love' 'belong (to)' 'know' 'want' 'resemble' and so on are 'stative' verbs. So, these verbs can NOT normally be used in the progressive form as in "I'm knowing him." "I'm belonging to the tennis club now." "I'm loving her so much." or "She is resembling her mother," when we refer to "states." Instead, we have to say "I know him." "I belong to the tennis club now." "I love her so much." or "She resembles her mother."

But I notice that the commercial phrase of a big worldwide hamburger shop is, as is probably well known, "I'm loving it." I believe this sentence is grammatically incorrect because 'love' is a stative verb. Therefore, this sentence should be like "I love it." Why does the burger shop use a seemingly ungrammatical expression? Could you please tell me the reason why? In addition, when I was reading a book the other day, I came across the sentence "I'm knowing it" which would normally be treated as ungrammatical. So, could you tell me what's going on in the sentences "I'm loving it" and "I'm knowing it"? I think that to answer this question would be to answer the difference(s) between simple forms of verbs and progressive forms of verbs. I would like you to give me your explanations.

ANSWER

🎧 55

Language is always in a state of flux and change. The changes are most often initiated by people that are not grammar teachers. In my opinion, this is unfortunate.

What we see in the case you offer is the desire by the users of the phrase to emphasize continuation in action. The owners of the burger restaurant chain want to emphasize that you will continue to enjoy their restaurants not only once but time and again. So, by using the phrase "I'm loving it," the shop owners can express their wishes that their customers will return indefinitely. "I'm knowing it" is a phrase that would normally be referred to as a case of ungrammatical English usage. However, what might the author of the book mean? Perhaps the author refers to a process of evolution. For example, we might not understand something completely but are getting there step by step. Examples that denote the gradual process of getting the picture of something would be *I am understanding it, I am grasping it,* or *I am knowing it*. Language changes and evolves and this could lead to the use of "I'm loving it" which has become part of regularly used English.

This adjustment and evolution in language also make the phrases given above somewhat normal. In a short while, when you look at an American English dictionary you will find phrases like "I'm loving it," or "I'm knowing it," and the authors will say that they are completely acceptable depending on the circumstances. This kind of change or evolution has already happened with nouns like "Google®" and it has become a verb as in "google it" or "googling."

Now let's consider the issue of the difference(s) between simple present verbs and present progressive verbs. A simple present verb is used in two situations: (1) when we give a fact or state something that is true in the present situation or (2) when we discuss repeated actions and habits. Let me give some examples.

In the case where we give a fact that is true in the present situation, we might say, "Sharks live in the sea," or "Greenland has glaciers," or, perhaps, "I study English in college." In each of these cases, the verbs "live," "has," and "study," are simple present verbs. In the case of expressing repeated actions or habits, we might say, "I eat at home every evening," "He only drinks orange juice," or "We go to work five days each week."

Normally, we use the present progressive verb form on two occasions: (1) when somebody is doing something or something is happening at the present moment, and (2) when we discuss something that is occurring soon. For examples of (1), we might say, "My teacher is waiting for the tests to be finished," "We are learning how to play tennis in physical education class," "It is raining now," or "I am painting the house." For examples of (2), we might say "I'm studying English next hour," or "I am shopping with Sue in an hour."

The main difference between the two verb forms is that we use the simple present form to denote things that are permanent or general, whereas we use the present progressive form to indicate events and circumstances that may change or that are temporary. For example, we use the simple present form to say that Hirotaka lives in Tokyo, and the present progressive form to say that Hirotaka is living in Tokyo right now. Going back to our "I love it," and "I'm loving it" situations, the "grammatical" phrase should be "I love it" but for impact and the sense of continuance, the advertiser has changed the grammar to allow for a use of present progressive form, and we are told "I'm loving it." To be sure, the use of "I'm loving it" can undoubtedly be assumed to be of some help to build the good relationship between customers and the burger shop.

Exercise 1

Choose the correct expression in each sentence.

1. The movie was very long and generally boring, but I must (admit / be admitting), the last scene was very moving.

2. I've started to learn Greek. Now (I'm knowing / I know) how difficult it is to understand the Greek language's complex grammar rules.

3. You say your proposal is the best and should be accepted. But I (refuse / am refusing) to agree with you.

4. (I'm certainly agreeing / I certainly agree) that his suggestion should be accepted.

5. I've finally saved enough money to travel abroad, so (I'm considering / I consider) visiting Italy, Spain and Portugal this summer.

6. (He had / was having) dinner when I called him up.

7. She (belongs / is belonging) to the tennis club.

8. Tom often comes to our place. Our kids (love / are loving) having him here.

9. Tom is with us now. Our kids (love / are loving) having him here.

10. I (find / am finding) it astonishing that he suddenly got angry that way.

Exercise 2

Complete the sentences using the words given in the square brackets and then translate them into Japanese.

1. I'm [moving, my, because, located, apartment, of, to, a, new, apartment, present, is, thinking, inconveniently].

   I'm _____ .

   Japanese _____

2. I'm [invest, lot, company, my, hasty, decision, to, a, money, in, regretting, that, of].

   I'm _____ .

   Japanese _____

3. As [better, got, her, liking, he, to, less, know, he, was, her, and, less].

   As _____ .

   Japanese _____

4. I [this, run, more, that, am, finding, and, the, roots, more, of, problem, deep].

   I _____.

   Japanese _____

5. A [idea, on, came, a, to, me, was, mathematics, I, while, book, reading, brilliant].

   A _____.

   Japanese _____

6. She [started, she, was, on, a, lose, diet, and, jogging, because, desperate, to, went, weight]

   She _____.

   Japanese _____

7. Just [to, walk, out, when, rain, I, was, hard, going, for, a, it, began].

   Just _____.

   Japanese _____

Exercise 3

Change the forms of the verbs given in the square brackets into correct forms.

1. As the years go by, he [resemble] his father more and more. [   ]

2. She [be] kind. What is she up to? [   ]

3. The sun [rise] in the east and [set] in the west. [   ]

   [   ]

4. He heard someone calling his name while he [take] a shower. [   ]

5. I [shout] with joy as I heard the good news. [   ]

Understanding English Grammar and Usage　　　　　[B-967]

英語の文法と語法を理解する

1　刷　　2024 年 2 月 26 日

著　者	Patrick Dougherty　　パトリック・ドーティー
	友繁 義典　　　　　　Yoshinori Tomoshige

発行者　南雲　一範　Kazunori Nagumo
発行所　株式会社　南雲堂
　　　　〒162-0801　東京都新宿区山吹町 361
　　　　NAN' UN-DO CO.,Ltd.
　　　　361 Yamabuki-cho, Shinjuku-ku, Tokyo 162-0801, Japan
　　　　振替口座：00160-0-46863
　　　　TEL：03-3268-2311(営業部：学校関係)
　　　　TEL：03-3268-2384(営業部：書店関係)
　　　　TEL：03-3268-2387(編集部)
　　　　FAX：03-3269-2486

編集者　加藤　敦

組　版　中西　史子

装　丁　銀月堂

検　印　省略

コード　ISBN978-4-523-17967-2　C0082

Printed in Japan

E-mail　nanundo@post.email.ne.jp
URL　　https://www.nanun-do.co.jp